BROKEN TREATY

by
STEVE FENTON

Copyright ©2011 by Steve Fenton.

All rights reseerved. This book,
or parts thereof, may not be
reproduced in any form without
permission from the publisher;
exceptions are made for brief excerpts
used in published reviews.

Published by
PDX Printing
100 Porfirio Diaz ST
El Paso, TX 79902

ISBN: 978-0-9838268-0-4

Printed in the United States

Table of Contents

Prologue 7
1. An alarming conversation 11
2. Diplomacy and legalities 23
3. A "routine" Christmas trip 33
4. Meeting Silvia: 12 years earlier 37
5. The tortilla king of Xalapa 45
6. Days Missing: 119 55
7. The tequila sisters and a bottle of hair dye
   (Days missing: 185) 63
8. A discreet note 77
9. Thanksgiving in Mexico City 87
10. The Vague Convention Treaty 97
11. time to do something 105
12. adopting a disguise 113
13. Let's bring Stephen home 119
14. The master plan 121
15. Losing our federale 133
16. A storm is coming 145
17. Remembering life before Spanish 161
18. The FBI Arrives 175
19. Melanie Headrick's call 185
20. Homecoming! 197
21. Back in California 209
22. Sisterhood of the pantalones 215
23. Back to school 225
24. Courts and Sports 235
25. The rattle of machetes 243
26. A visit through the border fence 253
27. Silvia returns to face the music 261

28. NO GOOD DEED GOES UNPUNISHED 271
29. STEPHEN'S REVELATION 281
EPILOGUE 285

Prologue

On October 1, 1991, Mexico joined the United States and many other countries as party to an international treaty providing for the speedy return of kidnapped children.

Known informally as "the Hague Convention," the name actually dates back to 1899 and applies to a litany of documents covering a variety of international agreements. As used in this book, the Hague Convention refers to "The Hague Convention on the Civil Aspects of International Child Abduction."

The treaty also provides for the speedy return of children held illegally in a country that is not their "country of habitual residence."

In signing and ratifying the treaty, diplomats and politicians agreed and understood that to avoid added trauma to a child, kidnapped children need to be returned home as soon as possible.

The Hague Convention thus provides a legal mechanism for international enforcement of the child custody arrangements in force before an abduction or illegal retention.

Treaty proponents were hopeful it would deter parents from moving a child from one country to another in hopes of finding more sympathetic courts. As of the summer of 2011, some 85 countries had signed and ratified the Hague Convention.

Is the treaty effective?

No, it is not, according to David Goldman, the parent of an abducted child, who says signatory countries routinely thumb their noses at the treaty.

On May 24, 2011, Goldman appeared before the U.S. House Committee on Foreign Affairs Subcommittee on Africa, Global

BROKEN TREATY

Health and Human Rights and offered the following testimony:

"The last three annual Hague compliance reports prepared by the State Department show that the total number of abducted American children for (the last three years) was 4,728." He added that the same reports "also show that (only) about 1,200 children were returned."

At the conclusion of his testimony, Goldman delivered to subcommittee members a letter addressed to Secretary of State Hillary Rodham Clinton. It was signed by 85 parents who were appealing to the secretary "for help as left-behind parents of 117 American children who have been abducted and remain unlawfully retained in 25 countries.

"We also represent a number of U.S. service members whose children were abducted while serving our country overseas," the letter said.

Among the worst non-complying countries, according to the U.S. State Department, is the Republic of Mexico. In its 2011 report to Congress, the State Department reported 329 new cases in 2010 involving 524 children. It is expected that only a fraction of the children will be returned. In its 2010 report for fiscal 2009, the Department noted that "in at least two instances, six months elapsed between the time the case was assigned to a court and the date of the first hearing; in another, seven months elapsed. In five other cases, it took between 16 and 55 months before the court held the first hearing on the application for return."

BROKEN TREATY

Such lengthy delays frequently lead to a court ruling that the children should not be returned because they have become "settled" in their new environment.

This book is the true story of an extraordinary effort by the father of one abducted child after he became convinced the Hague Convention was just a "Vague Convention," and that he would never see his son again unless he took matters into his own hands.

This also is the hair-raising story of how he managed to spirit his son out of Mexico, the aftermath, and how he and his son dealt with the many issues that followed.

Two first names have been changed to protect the individual's identity: Silvia and Alberto. All other names are real, as is the story.

BROKEN TREATY

BROKEN TREATY

Chapter 1

An alarming conversation

The telephone call that set off alarm bells came the evening of January 2, 1993, while I was at home in Los Altos, California. My wife Silvia had taken our 6-year-old son Stephen to visit her parents and family in southeastern Mexico. She was calling from Xalapa, in the state of Veracruz, to let me know that she would not be coming home as scheduled.

I had given her permission to take Stephen for a two-week visit over the Christmas holiday, while I stayed behind in California to continue my work as a contractor.

"We're going to stay a couple more weeks, Steve. My father's diabetes has gotten much worse, and I want to be with him," she said.

My chest tightened and a lump formed in my throat.

"That's not a good idea, Silvia. You did this last year but he missed only a few days of pre-school. Now you're asking to have him miss two weeks of kindergarten when you know he's behind in class."

"I've already taken care of that. I found an English-speaking school he can attend, so he won't miss anything," she explained.

The dialog had just taken a strange and abrupt turn. I turned the receiver over in my hand as though it might help me make sense of what I was hearing.

She had enrolled him in school in Mexico?

"You only had permission to take him for two weeks, not four.

BROKEN TREATY

I want you to get him back home by the original return date," I demanded.

"It's okay. We'll be home in two weeks," she said, showing no intention of backing down.

I knew that losing my cool over the phone would come back to bite me, so I held my tongue.

"Well, I guess I'll have to talk to the school and let them know. But if he's not back here in two weeks I'm coming down myself to bring him home!"

Having nothing more to say, she put Stephen on the phone.

"Hi, Dad," he said. I was relieved to hear him, but the usual cheer was gone from his voice. He began to express concern that his Mom was putting him into a strange school.

"I want to come home," he pleaded in a tone that was unusual. He always thought I could do anything. But at that moment I felt vulnerable. I couldn't offer a solution short of getting on a flight the next day to bring him home.

"Stephen, it's just going to be a couple more weeks. Mom is worried about her dad and wants to help out. I'll be waiting for you at the airport when you get off the plane. Just have a fun time for the rest of your visit, enjoy the food and let the family spoil you a little longer. I'll talk to Mrs. Picarello, when school starts on Monday," I said.

We talked small talk about his visit and he asked about Grandma and Grandpa, but I sensed that he remained apprehensive and alarmed.

"We'll talk again in a few days, Son," I said, offering what reassurance I could from nearly 2,000 miles away. I didn't feel good about the call. The thought that Silvia might try to keep him in Mexico crossed my mind, but I dismissed it thinking she couldn't possibly want to jerk Stephen out of school and pull him away from his friends and family in California.

Three days later I stopped by my parents' house in the evening. My father met me at the door with a worried look.

"Listen Steve, I have some bad news about Stephen. Silvia called Jerry at work (her boss, who also is an in-law) to say that she had made a difficult decision. She has decided to stay in Mexico and will not be returning to work. Jerry said he told her that he didn't understand what she was doing."

My father seemed to understand the implications of what he was telling me. I knew instantly what it all meant—Stephen wasn't coming home.

My heart sank like a lost anchor. Silvia could be pig-headed, and once she made up her mind to do something nothing could change it.

A scenario flashed through my head of me busting into the fortress-like compound of Silvia's family in Mexico to rescue Stephen. I realized how dire the situation was and that I had virtually no hope of convincing Silvia that this was a bad decision for everybody, especially our son.

I had a bad feeling about where this was headed. I couldn't help but think that Silvia's father Alberto had influenced her decision. My son's maternal grandfather had never completely come to terms with the fact that his favorite daughter had fallen in love with an American, gotten married and moved to California.

When I got on the phone to Xalapa, Silvia's mother answered

and told me Silvia was out. I tried to be calm and explained to her that international laws wouldn't permit Stephen to remain in Mexico, reminding her that Stephen was an American citizen. She was unimpressed and asked me to call back later.

Later that same evening Silvia took my call. I played ignorant and acted as though there was some confusion about her intentions.

"I've decided to stay in Xalapa with Stephen," she stated.

I chose my next words carefully. If she saw a blanket of threats, it would only get worse.

"You realize, don't you, that what you are doing is completely against the law? Stephen is an American citizen. I only gave you permission to take him for two weeks. Right now you are in violation of that agreement. I want you to book the next flight back to San Francisco with Stephen." It was a gamble but I hoped she would reconsider.

"I know a lot of mothers down here who have done this same thing with no problems," she countered. "Here the courts always order that the children go with the mother. We'll work something out in court so that you can spend some time with Stephen."

By now she had moved from defensive to defiant. I couldn't believe her brazenness. I asked to speak to Stephen and she handed the phone to him. He had apparently been listening to our conversation and had obviously just realized his mother's intention. During his six years of life I had never heard him sound scared, but now he had a tremble in his voice. As he began to speak I could tell he was near tears.

"Dad, I want you to come and get me now. I want to go home. I miss school and my friends. I want to finish the submarine with you.

BROKEN TREATY

I need you to come and get me now," he pleaded.

I could picture Stephen holding the phone with both hands at the small, decorative marble-top table where the household phone was located. He would be in a passageway between the living room and the bedrooms on the lower floor of Silvia's father's house. I could picture him discreetly looking away from Silvia while he urged me to come and get him.

I was going to bring my son home somehow; I just had to figure out what my options were and the most effective approach.

"Stephen, it's going to take a little while but I promise I will bring you home. Please, just know that I will come for you as soon as I straighten out some things here," I assured him. Silvia decided our conversation was over, took the phone from Stephen and hung up.

I took the rest of the week off from my business and pursued every recourse I could turn up. The next morning, a Tuesday, I was referred by the local police to the Santa Clara County District Attorney's office to file a report with the Child Abduction Unit.

My call was directed to a female investigator, Melanie Headrick. I told her what had happened and she responded with a series of direct questions, probing to determine if there had been any kind of abuse toward Silvia, Stephen or even myself.

My responses were prompt and emphatic.

"No abuse of any kind, whatsoever," I responded.

"Mr. Fenton, I highly recommend that you give your wife a chance to reconsider her position. In most cases the abducting parent soon realizes that it was not a good decision and ends up returning with the child," she offered.

BROKEN TREATY

"Ms. Headrick, my wife has made her decision. She has called her boss and quit her job. She's not coming back!"

My revelation seemed to trigger a more serious tone from Ms. Headrick.

"Then I think you need to come down to my office and file a statement. We can have one of our Spanish speaking investigators call the home in Mexico and put some pressure on her to return with the threat of a warrant if she doesn't comply. That sometimes is all it takes to get results," she said.

I felt good about the direction the conversation had gone and that I had made it through an initial screening. An appointment was set for the next day. But before our call ended, she also suggested I contact a non-profit organization called The Vanished Children's Alliance.

I called immediately and Gail Wood, a caseworker with the VCA, took my call. She listened sympathetically to my situation, and then offered some initial advice. Mexico, only the previous year, had become a signatory to the Hague Convention, an international accord stipulating the return of internationally abducted children back to their home country.

She recommended a number of attorneys including a world-renowned Hague Treaty specialist, Bill Hilton. I learned that Hilton was the best known expert in the field of international child abduction. In the space of one morning I received an education on international child abduction, while clinging to the hope that it was all unnecessary.

When I got to the Santa Clara County Child Abduction Unit the next day, I was seated in the reception area for only a few moments when Melanie Headrick came out to greet me with a smile. She wore her light-brown hair short, had gentle blue eyes and a button-nose. I felt comfortable with her.

She escorted me through a secured door and into her office. I assumed she had run a background check on me to see if there was any history of violence or abuse.

"Have you had any further contact with your wife or son since we spoke yesterday?" she asked.

"No, I've been trying to figure what my options are before I try to talk with her and Stephen again," I responded.

She seemed receptive to my dilemma and began to offer some insight. I listened carefully to every word that left her lips. I had an odd feeling that there was going to be a lengthy involvement on her part in trying to bring Stephen home.

"The first thing you need to do is establish in court that you are going to be the sole custodial parent. This will do two things: It will tell your wife that she will lose custody if she does not appear for the custody hearing; second, it will give you leverage in your Hague Convention case should it go that way. I recommend that you consult an attorney by the name of Bill Hilton. He's the best known in his field, and he only charges a fraction of what other attorneys demand who have much less experience," she told me. I realized that this was the same name that had been given me before by the woman at the VCA.

Melanie said she would arrange to have one of the bilingual investigators in the department call the home in Mexico and demand that Silvia immediately return Stephen or face a warrant for her arrest attached to a substantial bail.

BROKEN TREATY

As I sat giving details, my eyes drifted around her small office, noticing the faces of so many missing children. It could have been wallpaper.

"How many of these kids have you found," I asked.

"Every face you see is a child still missing. They only come down when one is recovered," she confided.

I stopped asking questions. When we finished, I left with a glimmer of hope that Silvia might see her decision as a bad one, returning with Stephen or at least releasing him to let me bring him home. It was distressing to think that I might see him in the "sea of missing faces."

Bill Hilton is a white-haired, mustached, tall man who doesn't own a car but operates his practice from his home, an old Victorian house near Santa Clara University campus, convenient to the Santa Clara County Superior Courthouse. I was advised that he was eccentric; he didn't really care what other people thought and that he made his own clothes. He was also reportedly estranged from the Hilton Empire, but most important to me: he was overwhelmingly revered by the courts for his expertise in the civil aspects of international child abduction.

Although his rates seemed reasonable, his $2,000 retainer cleaned me out, and I was informed I now had to prepare for a landslide of legal costs on both sides of the border. At his office I prepared a declaration describing Silvia's decision to keep Stephen in Mexico, now considered by authorities a "clear case of child abduction." His initial remarks were reassuring.

"The Hague Convention Treaty is a relatively new agreement between the U.S. and Mexico. I know quite well the Mexican counterparts in the Foreign Ministry that will be on the other end of this. The results have been somewhat discouraging regarding the return of abducted children out of Mexico. One thing you have in your favor is that your son has always lived in California and that will establish his 'habitual residence,' which is paramount in any case of this type. You have a very strong position no matter what your wife might try to claim," he explained.

I now had to ask a burning question.

"How long do you think it will take to get the authorities in Mexico to recover my son?"

"I'll begin working on the petition immediately. We could have cooperation from the Mexicans as soon as six weeks after filing the petition but there is no set timeline. Just know this: The worst thing you could do would be to go into Mexico and get involved in a custodial battle in the courts. If you did get involved, the Hague Convention Treaty would drop your case and consider it a local matter as you will have been inducted into the Family Court system in Mexico."

It was one thing to have the support of the court, but I saw the potential for the whole case turning into a long, international, open-ended legal test. My thoughts turned to the desperate voice of my son pleading to come get him. Not a moment passed that I didn't worry that he was thinking his Dad had forgotten him. There was no way he could know how complicated the whole scenario had become. I would bring him home, but it would take time and careful legal maneuvering both in the U.S. and Mexico.

I had intended to eventually travel to Xalapa to try and see Stephen once all the legal strategies were in place. But now I had to consider that a harmful move. Another consideration was money. I had used up valuable time from my job to get things moving. I needed to get back to work to start bringing in as much money as I could.

The Vanished Children's Alliance was the place I dreaded visiting most. I was reluctant to spend my time in a place where I was a "regular" with the other parents in this tragedy. I privately felt like a parental "loser," consumed with guilt that my son had seen no action from me.

The Vanished Children's Alliance operates through donations and grants with most of the staff made up of volunteers, organizing flyers, working with local police agencies and the FBI to help find and recover children domestically and abroad.

Gail Wood, the woman I had talked with on the phone, greeted and introduced me to some of the staff and volunteers. Their eyes were kind; in them I saw that they wanted to somehow share my loss. They met only a small percentage of the "left-behind parents." They helped many of their cases by combining resources with the National Center for Missing and Exploited Children.

The founder of the agency, Georgia Hilgeman, had her own daughter abducted to Mexico at the age of 18 months. Georgia is a forthright brunette with little patience for complacency. Her ex-husband had staged a phony kidnapping and sent their daughter to live with his parents in Mexico. Through her own relentless campaign and the help of a private investigator, she eventually discovered that her daughter was alive and living in the mountains of a small town in southwestern Mexico. She enlisted the help of some Spanish speaking contacts and paid a local policeman to assist in the rescue of her daughter. The husband was eventually convicted of felony child abduction, but served only 18 months in a California jail.

Almost in the same moment we exchanged greetings, she led me by the arm away from the other staff members in the group, out of earshot. Georgia was as serious as a heart attack.

"You are going to have to go down there yourself and bring your son home. The State Department isn't going to help you and the Mexicans have been terribly ineffective at sending any children back to the U.S. The Hague Treaty is nothing more than a good idea."

Georgia's words were like spurs into a tethered horse. I had tried to put the idea of pulling off some kind of rescue out of my mind in light of the diplomatic angles and the treaty. I had, in fact, in the last few days, developed some confidence in the local and international judicial systems. I believed I'd have to give the legal remedy a shot and had enlisted some devoted people in the short time since this all happened. It was clear to everyone that what Silvia was doing was immoral as well as criminal, but Georgia's echoing words stayed in my head. I couldn't help but wonder if she was well intentioned but simply misinformed and jumping the gun. I wanted to be my son's hero, with an unwrinkled cape and fresh dry-cleaned tights. I would first have to see what legal pursuits on both sides of the border could do, if anything at all.

I walked away from my first encounter with the Vanished Children's Alliance with mixed feelings, now even more uncertain of what it would take to get Stephen home.

BROKEN TREATY

Steve Fenton and Silvia during better days.
This photo was taken at their wedding in Xalapa.

's disappearance I left what once
Chapter 2

Diplomacy and legalities

Some months prior to Stephen's disappearance I left what once had been a lucrative real estate market as a Realtor. The market was in a slump and commission checks were becoming few and far between. I fell back on my first trade as a contractor. My business had supported Silvia and me before Stephen came along. But Hilton's retainer had cleaned me out, and I knew I'd just scratched the surface on the financial demands to come. I had new energy and drive to produce like never before. I wasn't quite sure what good the money I had allocated so far would do, but money seems to create activity in any quest.

The Vanished Children's Alliance had a volunteer named Sonya Wedin, a single mother in her late 40s pursuing a law degree. She learned about my plight and contacted me to offer her help. We arranged to meet and discuss my case at the VCA between her classes on a rainy Friday afternoon, only four days after Silvia's grim revelation. This was the last day I had free to talk to involved officials and support members during their regular work hours. Sonya explained to me that she couldn't represent me outright while still only a student, but offered to help with the court documents needed for court proceedings.

She knew all about Bill Hilton and considered him a legend in the civil aspects of international child recovery. She guided me in a declaration describing the chronological events since the day I drove Stephen and Silvia to the San Francisco International Airport for what was supposed to be a two-week visit. Within a week we were filing the appropriate papers in Superior Court.

Sonya became personally interested in my case and compassionate about Stephen's return. She expressed frustration at not yet being licensed to do more for me in the legal arena. I secretly believed that the onslaught of private interest in seeing Stephen home was a signal that it would eventually happen.

Meanwhile, I had been trying to reason with Silvia over the phone for several nights in a row after discovering her intention. I had gambled on taking a hard line, telling her I was going to the authorities here in California if she didn't return with our son immediately. In response, the line went dead and no one answered the phone in Xalapa the rest of that evening. Then, one night Stephen answered. Realizing his mother was not with him, I started to reassure him that I was working very hard to get him home as soon as possible, but before I could ask anything he began talking in whispers.

"Dad, Mom says we're not coming home, but I don't want to stay here. When are you coming to get me? You promised you'd come and get me. Remember?" he pleaded. His words opened new emotional wounds, but I could not let him hear the desperation in my voice.

"Don't worry Son, I'm coming for you, I just have to take care of a few things here in California before that happens," I replied.

I heard some commotion in the background and then Silvia's fury…"God damn it, Stephen!" she screamed.

Then the phone went dead. That was the last time I would ever talk to my son on the phone while he was in Mexico. His obvious

BROKEN TREATY

disappointment hit me like open-heart surgery without anesthesia.

My feelings alternated from being furious on the one hand to being helpless on the other. In the calls to Mexico that followed, anyone who answered the phone – whether servants or family members – said only that Silvia and Stephen "had left town." I just couldn't get my head around the concept of another human concealing a child from a parent.

I was convinced that Stephen was still at his maternal grandfather Alberto's house. The home was too convenient for Silvia – built like a fortress with heavy-gauge steel doors at the street entrance, and 10-foot-high concrete walls with broken glass imbedded at the top to discourage intruders. Homes in Mexico are built like that – something I found out the hard way while I was courting Silvia in Mexico. Unable to get anyone to come to the large steel doors at the street entry, I climbed over the wall, slicing my hands on the perpendicular glass shards.

Inside the home, Alberto had a small arsenal of handguns that he sometimes foolishly showed off. He once waved his pistol around inside a night club only to be jumped and pistol whipped with his own gun before being robbed. The attacker then took off with the gun. Alberto missed the weapon but bought another to replace it soon after.

I did get through to the home one last time, however. I insisted to a servant that I must speak to Alberto. This time he didn't duck the call. Along with his painfully raspy voice, he usually had a smirk on his face suggesting he knew something no one else did. I knew he would answer the phone with his smirk.

I was fluent in Spanish and at home with the smooth, clear

BROKEN TREATY

Veracruzan dialect. There was no need for pleasantries. He spoke:

"Why do you continue to harass this family when we tell you repeatedly that we don't know where your son and Silvia are?" Alberto insisted.

I took a second to compose myself before responding.

"Alberto, do you realize that what Silvia is doing is against the law not only in the United States but in Mexico as well? If Silvia does not return Stephen immediately, there will be legal issues including an arrest warrant for her." I waited for his reply.

"You can go to any authority you like but the fact is that the boy is the son of a Mexican mother and no laws will interfere with that," he said. "Silvia has decided to raise the boy here in Mexico." I didn't get a chance to respond before Alberto hung up.

Clearly, the man behind the raspy voice had established his position and announced his intentions. It was obvious to me that Alberto was behind the abduction of my son. Any reasoning that might have penetrated Silvia's defense of her actions would now be rebutted by a man who would help his daughter keep me from my son at any cost.

A Spanish-speaking investigator from Melanie Headrick's office followed up the next week and telephoned Alberto personally. Alberto claimed that neither he nor anyone else in the home had any knowledge of Stephen or Silvia's whereabouts. I considered that my hard line and the authorities' intervention had driven Silvia underground with Stephen.

With the necessary paperwork slowly coming together, my court proceedings on two fronts began to take shape: the local case in Santa Clara County Superior Family Court to establish that I would

BROKEN TREATY

have legal custody; and The Hague Convention petition to establish on an international level that Stephen's habitual residence was California. The legal and international diplomacy process was in its sixth week now and my contact with Stephen was long gone.

In late February of 1993, 45 days since Silvia's announcement, with three supportive sisters, my Dad, and Sonya Wedin looking on, I represented myself in Family Court as the petitioner and was awarded full custody of Stephen. The presiding judge asked whether I could represent that there was no abuse involved in Silvia's refusal to return to California. I looked the judge squarely in the eyes and in a firm voice responded.

"I represent to this court, that there has never been any abuse of any kind toward my wife or son." The clear intention in my voice left no room for doubt.

Under instructions I reluctantly requested a bench warrant for Silvia's arrest which he granted with no hesitation. The bench warrant was a formality to give greater power for authority involvement. I realized I had reached the "point of no return" as far as hoping for any reconciliation with Silvia. The judge also granted the District Attorney's office the right to use "any means at their disposal" to effect the recovery of Stephen. A significant step, but I realized that I was depending on paperwork to bring my son home. A custody order returns no hug.

We moved on to the filing of the Hague Treaty Petition. Bill Hilton went to work. He could now clearly establish that California was Stephen's "habitual residence" and although sole custody was never my intention, it gave greater leverage in the international aspect of the case with Mexico.

BROKEN TREATY

Much more had to be done; including pouring a small fortune into a certified document translator. The charge was by the word and costs piled up quickly. I had, through a contact in Xalapa, paid a retainer to an attorney to legally serve Silvia according to California's "due process," and also to act as an "agent for information" only. (This move would later jeopardize the entire Hague petition.) I was getting used to seeing my income evaporate as fast as I could generate it, but knowing that every dime I made brought me that much closer to seeing Stephen again made it worthwhile. I had taken on a side project working weekends now as well. I never grew tired though, since time spent working was much more constructive than the nervous pacing I'd have done otherwise.

D.A. investigator Melanie Headrick filed a criminal complaint charging parental kidnapping, a felony, and obtained an arrest warrant with a $500,000 bail. The Vanished Children's Alliance produced "Wanted" posters in both Spanish and English.

The VCA also offered weekly support meetings for parents of abducted children. I expressed my hesitation to Gail Wood, my support counselor, explaining that it would probably make me even more depressed to be surrounded by parents who were going through the same thing I was. She urged me to attend at least one meeting to see if I couldn't get something from it. I reluctantly agreed.

We all met around a large conference table at the VCA office on a wet Monday evening in late February. I was asked to give my story. For the first time I felt ashamed at losing my son, not knowing exactly how or when I would recover him, but certain that I would if it took my last breath. I listened to the others as they talked about their lost children. One man, whose wife took the kids to Ireland, had been trying to get them back for four years. Another had his daughters taken to Iran. Although he was able to trick his wife back to the U.S. to sign some legal paperwork, she did not bring the daughters. The wife was thrown in jail for contempt and sat for years unwilling to divulge the daughters' whereabouts. One woman had miraculously recovered her daughter from the Philippines when she finally got the State Department's attention. Another man by the name of Dave, approximately my age of 35, had his son taken to the Dutch West Indies in the Carribean. Dave had a powerful desire to be reunited with his 3-year-old son. I had the feeling that of all the parents at this meeting, he was most likely to see his child again. This was the case most similar to mine. I hadn't realized that fathers were so commonly the victims.

I absorbed a lot that night. I saw desperation as well as uncommon strength and hope in the faces of some traumatized parents. We had a common dilemma, and all of us were victims of extremely narcissistic and perhaps unstable spouses, but none had given up hope of seeing their child again. I took some comfort home that night, investing in persistence as a key to reunion.

"It's a matter of not losing hope," I told myself.

In mid March 1993, Melanie Headrick called my dad to explain that the Mexican Central Authority was expecting a local judge to recover Stephen at the home of Silvia's father in Xalapa. I was ecstatic. I had a euphoric surge of hope, grasping at the first forward movement to bring Stephen home.

It was painful to enter Stephen's room from the beginning, although I walked past his bedroom door countless times a day. His absence haunted me and demons taunted me with dreams of being reunited with Stephen. I would awaken feeling helpless and self-loathing. This went on night after night. I also became convinced that Alberto and Silvia were systematically turning Stephen against me. Imagining what hateful things they might be telling him would plunge me into dark fits of depression.

The room where he had spent his last night in the United States had been left untouched. Now I started to think about what was necessary for his return. I took the comforter and sheets from his bed and ran them through the wash. Two of my sisters, Mary and Karen, hearing news of the impending recovery, came over to help put his room in order and offer support.

One thing that had been explained to me by the Vanished Children's Alliance counselors was that parents of abducted children feel a "forever" loss as long as the children are gone. Conversely, parents who learned that their child had been killed suffered anguish and grief but, ironically, in these cases parents would find some degree of closure over time.

I went to bed on a Sunday night in early April of 1993 anticipating a call in the next day or two from the Mexican Central Authority authorizing Melanie Headrick to go immediately to Mexico City to bring my Son home. Protocol wouldn't permit me to bring Stephen home myself, nor could I be present. He could only be released to an official in California connected with the case. I wasn't happy about that. The two and a half months waiting for action seemed an eternity, but I could wait a few more days for the "diplomatic resolution" that would be returning Stephen home to California.

I gave everything demanded in the process, following the letter of the law. The Mexican government simply had to comply with the

BROKEN TREATY

Hague Treaty that it had signed. I worried most about how I could retain credibility with Stephen because it took so much longer than I had promised. I wrestled with what we would do first after he was home. Maybe we could start off with a fishing trip. I wanted at least a few mental health days free from school and work for us both before picking up old routines. I also wondered how many flights behind Stephen Silvia would be coming to manage her mess.

BROKEN TREATY

Stephen sharing with a friend.
This photo was taken in Xalapa during one of the twice-a-year visits.

Chapter 3

A "routine" Christmas trip

I knelt down on one knee in front of Stephen to get his attention. The 5-year-old boy with the island-sized brown eyes stopped pecking away at the keys of his Game Boy, punched "pause" and surrendered his attention. The departure gate was getting ready to begin boarding and the passengers began to line up. Most of the passengers were traveling to Mexico to be with family for the holidays; the flight had booked up two months in advance.

"I'll be calling Christmas Eve and again on New Years to check in on you. Santa will find you in Xalapa and there may be some gifts for you when you get back as well," I told Stephen.

"Dad, just promise me that you won't work on the submarine until I get back. We can load the missiles together. I know exactly how we left it and I'll know if you work on it," Stephen said in an almost adult tone.

"It will be just as we left it when you get back, I promise. Have fun, but listen to your Mom. You'll be back in two weeks, right before school starts again," I added, pulling him to me for a hug.

Stephen resumed playing his Game Boy. I let him have this Christmas gift early, knowing it would occupy him during the five-hour flight to Mexico City. I had also packed our favorite Jimmy Buffett tape in case he got homesick. The cassette had some of our favorite songs on it; namely "Volcano" and "Fins" that we played every morning on his way to kindergarten. I now turned to Silvia, just a few feet away, who was readying her carry-on bags to board the plane. Despite the difficulties of our separation, I still found her attractive in her slender jeans, blue sport coat, and brilliant white open-collar silk shirt. She is a petite woman, only 4-feet-10 and under 100 pounds. I gently took her by the arm and led her out of Stephen's earshot.

"Silvia, I've been thinking a lot about us. I want you to give some thought about trying to work things out--that is if you want to give it a chance," I said.

I don't know what compelled me to mention it at this moment. It just seemed like a good time and something to think about while she and Stephen were gone.

"You know Stephen would love to see that," I added, not expecting any kind of commitment. She didn't take long in responding and didn't seem at all surprised that I brought it up.

"I will think about it and tell you what I think when I get back," she said responding in flawless English; accentuated with her slow Veracruzan drawl. She didn't make eye contact.

Her response was about what I expected; not much interest. But I was sincere. We'd been separated for nearly two years and had never got around to talking about a divorce. I suppose that deep down, I figured we could eventually work things out. But we had moved in separate directions and the only thing we had in common now was our son, Stephen. I must confess that he seemed pretty well adjusted to our split knowing that he was the most important thing in our lives no matter what issues came between me and his mom.

Silvia never tampered with my relationship with Stephen. We had worked out a mutually agreeable custody arrangement, split right down the middle, without getting attorneys involved. It seemed to be working well, though I had never believed the separation would be permanent.

I watched the handsome young boy in the black "Giants" baseball jacket and his mother enter the departure gate. I waved until the two disappeared into the gangway to the plane.

Driving back home from the airport in the chilly San Francisco night, I felt a little depressed with the notion of spending another Christmas without my son. It was important, though, that he get plenty of exposure to the Mexican half of his heritage and hopefully pick up a little Spanish. He hadn't yet found much need for a second language. His mom was there to translate anything of interest to him. Her entire family doted over him.

I told myself the time would pass quickly, that Stephen would be back before I knew it. Still, home seemed so lonely when he was gone. Just walking past his bedroom door, knowing how far away he was made my heart heavy. But I would survive. In two weeks I'd be back into my routine of nagging Stephen to get his homework finished – I reassured myself.

BROKEN TREATY

Stephen on a fishing trip with his Dad before the abduction.

Chapter 4

Meeting Silvia: 12 years earlier

I met Silvia within the first two weeks of enrolling at the University of the Americas in Puebla, Mexico, as a foreign student studying International Relations. It was the only university south of the border that could boast being U.S. accredited. In the school cafeteria we were introduced by a girl coincidently from my hometown of Los Altos, California. Sally Dale was her name and Silvia was her roommate. This was Silvia's first time away from home and Sally told me privately that she cried herself to sleep at night the entire first week because she missed her family in Xalapa, Veracruz, a three-hour bus ride from the University.

Captivated by Silvia's stunning beauty, I wondered how such fine features could have been engineered into such a petite girl. She had shoulder-length, wavy brown hair, perfect golden skin, coffee brown eyes, a tiny nose and a smile that showed off her small round cheeks. The young lady had charm in spades, letting her natural beauty speak volumes. Her smile and eyes were so seductively brilliant I was overwhelmed. Yet I discovered she was painfully shy. My early fumbling at Spanish assured her of endless entertainment. While my course of study included two hours of intensive Spanish every day, the one-on-one interaction with Silvia fast-forwarded my fluency. I'd enjoyed some attention as the "guero"— (blondie) from the local women, but it wasn't long before I began an exclusive relationship with Silvia.

Silvia's background was about as traditionally Mexican as one

BROKEN TREATY

could be, yet she seemed to enjoy my fresh, sometimes downright immature antics. I liked showing off to get her attention. One day I skateboarded through the middle of Cholula, a small town near campus. I was holding a rope tied to the bumper of my old pickup truck in one hand and a can of "Tecate" beer in the other. My buddy Malcolm from Del Mar drove and Hector from Chicago rode shotgun. We created a scene, moving through an intersection to pass in front of the restaurant where Silvia was having lunch with girlfriends, winning a huge roar from the group as they watched me go by, but Silvia only blushed and hid her face.

Although only students of International Relations, on occasion we conferred upon ourselves honorary diplomatic immunity. One Saturday afternoon we learned that then President Portillo would be passing through town in a motorcade. My friends and I decided to get a close look at the procession. Ludovic Bois, a tall and loveably pompous but debonair classmate from Paris, had an old blue ragtop Pontiac that he brought down from Texas. Gilbert, from Belize, produced two small flags, one American and another Mexican that we planted on the two front corners of the hood. We decided to see how close we could get to the action, and we ended up less than 20 feet behind the president's bus in the middle of the motorcade. Ludovic had no opportunity to get off the motorcade route with city onlookers crowding the sidewalk.

Budget entourage! I sat up on the back seat of the large convertible in jeans and a tank top shirt, and began waving to the crowd like a celebrity. Along with French and American representation, Gilbert from Belize blew kisses to the Pueblan girls, rounding up our multinational ragtop procession through a dozen city blocks of

BROKEN TREATY

Puebla, following the motorcade until we arrived at the airport.

We drew more attention than the president's bus. Luckily no one saw us as a threat – more of a curiosity; the weaponized soldiers posted along the route seemed perplexed, but the school children, assembled in school uniforms on the motorcade route to greet the president, loved us.

On the flip side of my playfulness, I had a bag full of ideology that didn't quite fit the culture, creating occasional issues with Silvia. I had a tendency to face any challenge that crossed my path head-on.

As a cocky American, I was often targeted by corrupt cops. Any interaction with them usually entailed forking over hard-to-come-by-pesos on a modest student budget. I hated giving out bribe money, and Silvia grew impatient with my arguing with cops rather than giving them money that could buy us a good meal in town. Once, after I accidentally ran a red light, a transit cop jumped in a taxi and came after me. As I got out of my truck the cop pulled out his citation booklet.

"Running a red light is a serious infraction in Cholula," he lectured.

"I'm sorry I just didn't notice the traffic light," I replied.

The scene drew the attention of pedestrians and passing traffic during the siesta hours of the warm spring afternoon. The cop grew a little nervous with so many onlookers now stopping to watch.

"We can take care of this matter for fifty pesos," the cop suggested discreetly.

"I would prefer that you give me a citation instead," I replied.

He opened up his citation book and lifted his pen, but before writing anything he paused and looked at me.

BROKEN TREATY

"How about just enough for a coke?" he suggested.

I declined. I could see that he'd never actually written a ticket. A small crowd had gathered by now. The cop realized he wasn't going to get anything out of me; too many witnesses. Somewhat humiliated, he climbed back into the taxi and left. I had a sneaking suspicion that the taxi driver was going to get stiffed.

Silvia, instead of being impressed with my righteous demonstration, became furious.

"That was about the stupidest thing I've ever seen. If this had happened at night, that cop could have robbed and killed us both with no fear of prosecution. He's going to put the word out about the smart ass "gringo" driving around town in the yellow truck with black trim and the California plates, probably the only vehicle like it in Mexico.

"Steve, these cops have long memories and this cop will be looking for an opportunity to settle a score for making him look like an idiot – all for the price of a soda?" Silvia scolded.

That was my first reprimand in Spanish. I knew my language skills were improving because I didn't have to ask her to repeat anything. Silence filled the cab of my truck as we drove down the frontage road toward our dorms on campus. Now I was the one who felt humiliated.

While for me it was a matter of principal, it simply didn't make sense to Silvia. Mexicans want little to do with the police, whom they view as little more than criminals with guns and a badge. A remittance to a policeman here and there is just part of life in Mexico. I had a lot to learn about "my attitude in the lower latitude."

One Saturday night while Silvia had gone back to Xalapa to

BROKEN TREATY

spend the weekend with her family, I was invited to the grand opening of a night club in Cholula by the owner, an entrepreneurial fellow student and friend named Alejandro. The club was called "Las Yardas," named for the three-foot-tall beer glasses that were designed to rest in a slot at your table. The place was alive with dancing, and music drifted out into the cool evening. The students weren't very popular with the local "poblanos," the elite younger crowd that seemed to enjoy the wealth and clout of their family names. They were pretty bold about walking around with a gun tucked in their waistbands and we gave them a wide birth.

That evening while helping celebrate the grand opening, I overheard some heated arguing between an attractive young blond woman and a man sporting a black leather jacket and designer jeans —one of the Poblanos. The place was dim, but I could see the man trying to pull the woman toward the entrance. She was trying to pull away from him. Instinctively, I moved toward them. I grabbed the man's wrist and pulled his hand away from the girl's arm.

"I don't think she wants to go with you," I said, causing him to crane his neck around to see who had the audacity to interfere. Then he simply glared at me in disbelief and without a word walked away. The young woman gave me a surprised look and then thanked me for coming to her aid.

"Why don't you sit down with me and have a drink?" she invited.

As she spoke I realized that she wasn't Mexican. She said she was the daughter of a German engineer employed at the Volkswagen plant in Puebla. I was studying German now as a third language and spoke to her a little in Deutsch, though Spanish dominated our dialogue. She'd never met an American.

"What did that guy want anyway?" I asked.

"He's my boyfriend's cousin. He thought it was disrespectful for me to be here without him. He wanted to take me home," she said.

"I'm lucky it didn't turn into a brawl," I said laughing.

At that moment the Poblano in the leather jacket with two others walked up behind us.

"We'd like to talk to you outside," he motioned toward the entrance.

"Sorry, but I don't like the odds; you'll have to dance with each other," I replied.

Backing down from a fight was not an idea I liked, but I had a feeling that these guys planned to use more than fists. The three men scowled down at me, then walked away.

Fifteen minutes later, I said goodbye to the girl to go find Ludovic who had come to the bar with me; but first a men's room visit. Now, standing at the urinal in the men's room, I heard the door open and close behind me. Only seconds later the door opened again and I heard a scuffle. Alejandro, the bar owner, had realized what was about to happen and rushed into the restroom. He had the Poblano pinned, one knee across the man's chest and another across his elbow, and was trying to wrestle a gun out of the man's hand. Alejandro was screaming at me to leave the night club "ahorita!" — "now!"

I saw the snub-nose revolver still in the Poblano's hand. It was a safe assumption that he was going to shoot me in the back. I clambered over the two, managing a terrified nod to Alejandro, who had probably just saved my life. I bolted through the crowd catching the eyes of Ludovic who'd figured out by now the trouble I'd found for myself. My concern now was – as I crashed through the exit with Ludovic – if the other two goons would be waiting for me outside. We made it to my truck and sped off toward the safety of the campus dorms.

The incident had me pretty shaken up and it made me take a good look at my imported virtues in a country that made the American Wild West look like a tea-and-crumpet get-together.

Before I had a chance to tell her, Silvia learned about the incident from mutual friends. She couldn't understand the concept of getting involved in someone else's issues. After a raging lecture in a language I didn't know could be spoken so fast, Silvia announced that we were through. I thought I had lost her.

I was overwhelmed with remorse. I did my best with flowers and cards, wit and charm, but nothing seemed to get her attention. I began to seriously consider that it was all over. I had never come across a woman with such determination. "She was the woman for me," I told myself.

Only three semesters into my schooling in Mexico, I made a decision. I would ask Silvia to marry me.

BROKEN TREATY

Chapter 5

The tortilla king of Xalapa

Silvia's father, Alberto, was a colorful character; a traditional, conservative Mexican, short and balding, with a tooth missing here and there despite the fact he could well afford to replace them. He'd spent a couple of years in Chicago as a young adult and learned some English. He practiced every chance he got; his gravelly voice afflicted from a lifetime addiction to Marlboro Reds. I was patient when he spoke, remembering those who had been patient with me when I began my own struggle to learn Spanish.

He had built a family business, owning and operating a string of neighborhood micro tortilla factories. He had an eagle-eye for buying-out competitors. He was respectfully referred to as "the tortilla king." The tortilla is as vital to the Mexican diet as rice in Asia. As with gasoline and other essentials, the cost of tortillas per kilo is government regulated. Entrepreneurs in the tortilla industry are business savvy, operating on a tight profit margin. The owner's constant demons are work-related injuries. Along with the potential for limb-loss and explosions from the natural gas-driven conveyor furnace system, there is a large boiling vat for the maiz. The body of Alberto's manager was discovered one morning face down in one of those vats. Most of his flesh had boiled off.

Alberto was very possessive of Silvia. She was the prettiest of his four daughters and he often proclaimed her his favorite. He didn't handle well my request for his blessing to marry Silvia. The single saving consideration to him was that I was raised Catholic, even attending a parochial school run by nuns in my youth. Seeking guidance, he went on an all-night drinking binge to consort with his "compadres." They must have approved because he reluctantly gave in and a large wedding was planned.

At this point the logical thing for me to do was to leave the university and head back to California to find a way to support Silvia and me after we were married. My family was floored by my announcement, and worried that I hadn't thought things out. My sister Mary, convinced I'd lost my senses, insisted on meeting me in Mazatlan on my drive back to California as a chance to reason with me. We spent a few days immobilized as "beach potatoes" drinking ice-cold Dos Equis beer and gorging on boiled shrimp. Eventually, she saw things my way.

Once back in California, I put college on hold and began trying to figure out how to support a bride. I learned the San Jose Police Department was seeking bilingual officers. I passed all the tests with flying colors, including the Spanish bilingual four-person-panel verbal exam, but flunked the background check. Unbeknownst to me, one of my sister's under-aged boyfriends had used my birth certificate to obtain a driver's license so he could buy alcohol. When I couldn't explain the discrepancy in an interview, I was disqualified. However, a brother-in-law helped me get an apprentice carpenter's position with union benefits.

I had to commit to a couple of special requests from Alberto to compensate for the loss of his daughter: Silvia was to finish her college degree, and we would make at least two trips a year to Xalapa to spend time with her family over the holidays and again in summer. I would see to it that his requests were honored,

BROKEN TREATY

but I wondered if Alberto somehow mistakenly believed I was independently wealthy.

The wedding was spectacular, performed at 8:00 in the evening in a 200-year-old cathedral in the city square with 200 guests. The cathedral was breathtaking; four-story ceilings with brilliantly colored stained glass. Outside a light rain fell. Silvia was radiant in her perfect white gown as she floated through the towering ancient wooden doors.

I was terrified, having to read aloud from the Bible in Spanish, unfamiliar with many of the words. I stumbled nervously, bringing laughter from the crowd. The ceremony and glamorous reception that followed had the town talking for days. Alberto, though, drank so much brandy the night before that he completely humiliated himself in front of my family at dinner, causing him to nearly miss the wedding. The morning of the wedding, a doctor had to be called to the house to get him well enough to attend the ceremony.

Within a week Silvia and I flew to California to make our new life together. She had never been to the United States and I loved being with her as she saw the wonders of a first-world country. She marveled at the smooth roads, the courteous motorists, and the clean landscape. Within a month I had Silvia enrolled in junior college. I taught her how to catch the bus from our modest apartment in nearby Sunnyvale. She didn't speak English yet but I was confident she would pick it up quickly with English as a second language courses. I resumed my studies attending night courses after work. I changed my major to economics as studies in international relations were no longer practical.

We settled into a comfortable routine, with Silvia learning

BROKEN TREATY

English in great strides and both of us slowly working toward our degrees. I taught her to drive, allowing her to drop me off at the jobsite in the mornings and then get herself to classes, offering her some freedom and independence.

Over a year had gone by when a sudden back injury on the jobsite put me on disability and our modest lifestyle started to take some serious financial hits. Workman's compensation helped us barely get by. While in a rigorous physical therapy program I took some more college courses, trying to make the best use of my time.

I continued to honor Alberto's request to make the twice yearly visits back to Xalapa, for the holidays and summer, though the travel costs meant a tight budget. My only regret was that I couldn't get Silvia to leave her parent's house once we arrived. I wanted to travel around; maybe up to Puebla where we met, or Mexico City, but she wouldn't budge, explaining that "it would be disrespectful to her father," to leave the house. I did however have a few Mexican college buddies in town and, despite Silvia's disapproval, would get out with the boys once in a while.

Alberto's treat was to take the family to the port city of Veracruz and stay at a coastal resort called Chachalacas. One evening during a family dinner at the resort; with the influence of a few rounds of cocktails, Alberto suddenly instructed the entire family to go to their rooms at the hotel, but asked me to stay. Without uttering a word, Silvia's mother led Silvia, her three sisters and brother away into the mild evening breeze toward the hotel. As he often did with me, when reaching a certain level of intoxication, Alberto began a slurred attempt at English.

"Steve, you have been married to my daughter for three years now.

BROKEN TREATY

I think you are a good husband, almost like a son to me. I want to show my appreciation to you for taking such good care of Silvia," he told me.

I felt somewhat sheepish, thinking he was about to present a lavish gift. Maybe something on the caliber of the heavy gold Rolex he was never without; so heavy it seemed, that I could swear he listed to one side when he walked. His speech returned to Spanish.

"Steve, I want to buy you a woman tonight – one for each of us. I only pay for the most attractive women," he proudly confided. I performed an instant review of key words I thought I'd just heard to assemble my reply. This was going to be good story one day, but I needed to come up with a clever response that would get me out of the tight spot, yet not offend Alberto.

"Alberto, this is a very kind gesture but I should let you know that your daughter is the only woman for me. I simply couldn't live with myself knowing I cheated on Silvia," I offered.

He ignored my words and demanded that the waiter send the maître'd over. A moment later, the two had an agreement. A wad of paper pesos were stuffed into the maitre'd's hand. As the man headed away to fulfill the agreement, I had an idea.

"Alberto, let's order a couple more rounds of drinks while we're waiting and drink to the family, all here together again," I insisted.

I asked the waiter under my breath to make our drinks "doubles" of Coke and brandy. Alberto was diabetic and sensitive to alcohol, but once he started he couldn't stop until he vomited and passed out; sometimes in reverse order. I kept raising my glass for a toast and Alberto met every hoist. It wasn't until now, I realized, that the brandy was beginning to undermine Alberto's less than noble proposition. When the two women showed up 30 minutes later, Alberto became obnoxiously indignant to the maitre'd, complaining that they were not his caliber. They were though, surprisingly attractive; more along the lines of what my impression of a "call girl" might be. He shoved hundreds of dollars in pesos at the shocked man to send them away.

The bittersweet comfort of not having to hurt anyone's feelings and being thoroughly entertained while not leaving my seat was all I could have asked for. The thought had occurred to me that perhaps this was all some kind of test to confirm my loyalty to Silvia, masterminded by Alberto. But Alberto was careful with money. I had to figure that it was an alcohol infused impulse that drove Alberto to make such an outrageous gesture.

After handling the tip, I walked Alberto back toward the hotel, where loved ones waited and most likely feared the worst. Alberto swayed like a hammock on a tossing ship. He no longer tried to speak in English; or Spanish for that matter. He just set a course down the long terracotta-tile breezeway, looking for a door that might match the fuzzy numbers on his room key. I followed directly behind him, catching him occasionally as his world wobbled about. We found his door, and his wife opened and pulled Alberto into the room. She was quite relieved that the evening had gone no further than an impending hangover.

The next morning Silvia and I walked along the empty beach. Believing that we kept no secrets, I ventured to mention the "call girls" and bizarre events after her dad sent everyone away from the table. Instead of shock and disbelief, she kept her pace through the sand.

BROKEN TREATY

"We don't talk about these things," she calmly responded, not offering even a brief glance up at me that might offer a portal into her true feelings. She wasn't going there. We never discussed the matter again.

Day's later, back at Alberto's fortress-like home in Xalapa on New Year's Eve, another strange event occurred. While the family and some friends celebrated into the early hours of the morning, Alberto got liquored-up and disappeared from the party. When he rejoined the family, he had his 9 mm Beretta in his hand, making inaudible comments in my direction, but strangely avoiding eye contact. His speech was slurred, but the contempt in his piercing, almost black eyes was unmistakable when I finally drew his look. I assumed that he was headed outside to unload a clip into the air as is customary on New Year's Eve in Mexico. Instead, he began to wave the gun at me until some family members surrounded and disarmed him. No one in the family talked about the incident after that but a good friend of Alberto told me that he held some pent-up resentment toward me for taking his favorite daughter away from him.

My relationship with Alberto cooled significantly after that. I told Silvia it was time to head back to California, but she refused, not wanting to offend her father. There was no confusing where she placed her loyalty. I spent the rest of that holiday visit in Xalapa reading my books in a quiet corner of the living room, anxious to get back to California. Alberto never apologized for waving the gun, nor did anyone try to offer a worthy explanation. I believed that the incident exposed some underlying resentment that nobody in the family was willing to talk about, not even Silvia.

BROKEN TREATY

When Silvia revealed that I would be a father, I was understandably apprehensive at the notion of being a young parent and the dramatic change ahead. It was not that I thought the baby would be an intrusion into our lifestyle, but rather whether I could provide everything that a new life would need. I had only earned an associate degree and still had two semesters to go for an undergraduate degree.

I sought the wisdom of an expert – my father – who had sired nine children with my mother.

"If we'd all waited for just the right time to become a parent, not many of us would be here," dad commented.

He had a point. Besides all of his children had become remarkably successful.

Within 48 hours of learning about the baby, I embraced the responsibility, resolving to be a good father.

In September of 1986, Stephen was born at Stanford Hospital. Alberto had insisted that our son be given his name, but I pulled rank at the last moment when the birth information was needed, giving Stephen my name instead. Alberto couldn't publicly be offended considering that it is customary in Mexico for a father to assign his own name to the first son.

Our son was a blend of my lighter skin but with his mother's more exotic features of brown hair and large coffee eyes. From the first breath at birth, I understood the pride of bringing another life into our world. Except for the continued travel to Mexico, we were content being homebodies, finding each day in his development more precious than the last.

I kept busy with my business, and once again put my studies on hold. School could wait until I wasn't so busy. Besides, the new

BROKEN TREATY

demands of a baby made tuition a luxury beyond our budget. By the end of Stephen's first year, Silvia had gone back to school. Old enough for daycare in his second year, she managed a part-time job with an electronics firm while maintaining a part-time course load at school. Between the two of us we were able to get Stephen to and from daycare.

Impatient for Stephen to become my fishing partner, I'd set up his playpen beside me while fishing for striped bass at a reservoir. By age 3, he was learning to cast a line. He could land a fish by himself at age 4. Anything we caught he insisted on cooking up that night. In the evenings, there was always the time before going to sleep that I lay next to him to read aloud. A new story always inspired another favorite to keep me reading. He never tired of the same images or hearing the unchanged narration, always finding something new in his favorites each night. I treasured these times and hated to think they would eventually fade away, just as the nights watching him sleep in his crib were pages in our history.

While the bond between Stephen and me grew stronger with each day in his first few years, my union with Silvia began to crumble. Most of our common friends were Latino, a natural draw, as the language and culture made Silvia more comfortable. However, over the years, nearly every meaningful friendship with other couples was eventually undermined from jealousy or gossip. I never completely understood if the problems could be attributed to Silvia's pride or social complications. I'd become good friends with people from all over Mexico and nearly every country in Central and South America. The exposure kept my Spanish fresh as a welcome side effect, but in each instance, Silvia complained that her friends were saying things behind her back.

Around the time that our marriage began to chill, she became close with a local group from her home town in Xalapa, attending frequent gatherings. I thought that the connection to her hometown group would ease her apparent disenchantment with life in California. Instead, she became more isolated. I never saw good cause to recommend it, but unlike most green card transplants – to Silvia, the idea of becoming a U.S. citizen was absurd. Her loyalty lay with Mexico and her family. California would always be foreign soil.

We drifted further apart, eventually sleeping in separate rooms.

In the fall of 1990, while I was away on a fishing trip in Cabo San Lucas, Mexico, Silvia suddenly took Stephen and moved out of the home and into an apartment with a girlfriend from her home town. I was devastated. Although she had carefully organized the move in advance, I never saw it coming. I came home and they were gone.

We spent the next six months going to counseling for help, but Silvia's heart wasn't in it. There was never a dispute over legal or physical custody for Stephen. We respected each others parenting interests.

After the separation I no longer accompanied Stephen with Silvia on the semi-annual visits to Xalapa, but I never would have dreamed of denying her permission to take our son. As was our routine for the holidays, I provided a notarized statement to Silvia, authorizing her to take Stephen for a two-week visit to Veracruz. It was the week before Christmas 1992.

CHAPTER 6

DAYS MISSING: 119

Two days after Mexican authorities planned to pick up Stephen in early April of 1993, I received a faxed report from the International Child Abduction division of the State Department in Washington, D.C. It stated that when a local judge, a woman by the name of Juana Luna Sagreda, had gone to Alberto's house with police officers to recover my son, Alberto had met them at the front entry and declared not to know the whereabouts of Silvia or Stephen. Judge Sagreda had then sent the paperwork back to the Mexican Central Authority in Mexico City.

In a response to the State Department fax, I asked if the home had been searched for my son, and learned that the police never entered the home. Although I had spoken often to my State Department contact, Elizabeth Wadium, I seemed to get pre-scripted explanations to my questions. Every step seemed to follow strict diplomatic guidelines, sterilized of any meaningful encouragement. I couldn't seem to talk her into getting tough with our Mexican counterparts.

Eventually, Ms. Wadium grew weary of my repeated phone calls. When she learned I spoke fluent Spanish, she gave me the direct phone number to the Mexican Central Authority. She urged me to speak directly with them, which I was only too happy to do. I might have the luxury of cutting out the middle man, hopefully with less time wasted on diplomatic protocol. I would be courteous but direct. I soon established a working relationship with Laura Duclaud, a senior caseworker on the Mexican Authority end, who became my direct pipeline for information and was much more helpful than the U.S. State Department. In late April, she told me that new orders for Stephen's pickup were being prepared which included instructions to search the home. These papers would be sent to a local judge in Xalapa for execution.

Trying to hold my depression at bay, I embraced any positive news, trying to keep hope alive. When it came right down to it, I realized deep down that I was pinning my hopes on a legal process with little history of delivering. I just didn't know what else to do.

My hopes were raised again when I heard that Mexican authorities planned to search Alberto's home. Alberto just might take a look at the seriousness of the situation and consider what lay ahead in terms of hiding Stephen. Mexican pride, however, can be formidable; the threat of a house search might drive the family to become even more cunning at hiding Stephen.

I told Melanie Headrick about the next pickup attempt for Stephen. In a series of phone calls to Mexico City, she would become the designated U.S. authority to travel to Mexico to accompany Stephen back to California; however, protocol stipulated that I couldn't go to Xalapa. I would have to wait in Mexico City. I felt it only appropriate that I be present. Having Stephen taken to Mexico City by strangers didn't sit well with me. Still, I would have to wait in Mexico City.

Another six weeks went by before the next pickup would be attempted. It was now into May. My stomach gnawed at me day and night. I wasn't eating properly and started losing weight, obsessing on all the pieces that had to come together for a recovery. In the back of my mind I couldn't help but think of the influence, power and money Alberto had in his corner. The Mexican Central Authority was usually closed by the time I got home from work. I often couldn't make necessary international phone calls during work hours. During these times, my father, Tom, was instrumental in keeping my pipeline open with anyone who had a significant role.

On the day of the second scheduled pickup by authorities at the Xalapa home, there were no calls, only a fax from Eduardo Peña's office, the senior official overseeing my Hague case in Mexico. The fax, in poor English, follows:

SECRETARY OF FOREIGN RELATIONS
DATE: JUNE 1, 1993
SUBJECT: STEPHEN FENTON
THIS ACKNOWLEDGES RECEIPT OF YOUR FAX DATED MAY 20, 1993, REGARDING THE HAGUE PROCEEDINGS FOR THE RESTITUTION OF YOUR Son STEPHEN.
IN THIS REGARD, IT IS IMPORTANT TO STATE THE FOLLOWING:
1. THE MEXICAN CENTRAL AUTHORITY WAS ACTUALLY TAKING THE NECESSARY STEPS TO OBTAIN A COURT ORDER FOR THE RESTITUTION OF STEPHEN TO THE UNITED STATES.
2. THE SEVENTH FAMILY JUDGE OF THE STATE OF VERACRUZ, LIC. JUANA SAGREDO LUNA, WAS SUPPOSED TO ISSUE THE AFORESAID ORDER. IN ACCORDANCE WITH MEXICAN LAW, "A JUDICIAL ORDER CANNOT BE ISSUED IF THE RESPONDENT HAS NOT BEEN GIVEN THE OPPORTUNITY TO DEFEND HIMSELF DURING THE

RESPECTIVE PROCEDURE. THE INDIVIDUAL MUST BE NOTIFIED IN PERSON.

3. NEVERTHELESS, AND OWING TO THE SPECIAL CIRCUMSTANCES OF THIS MATTER, THE SAID FAMILY JUDGE WAS ADVISED NOT TO SUMMON MRS. FENTON BY THE AGENTS OF THE LOCAL SYSTEM FOR THE DEVELOPMENT OF THE FAMILY (DIF), WHO WERE SUPPOSED TO TAKE STEPHEN INTO THEIR CUSTODY FROM THE MOMENT IN WHICH THE RESTITUTION ORDER WAS ISSUED.

4. MEXICAN AUTHORITIES WERE NOT ABLE TO TAKE THOSE ACTIONS, DUE TO YOUR IMPRUDENT ATTITUDE OF CONTRACTING A LAWYER IN MEXICO FOR THE RECOVERY OF STEPHEN. THE ACTIONS TAKEN BY YOUR LAWYER PREVENTED MRS. FENTON FROM THE HAGUE PROCEEDINGS PROVOKING HER FLIGHT.

5. THE HAGUE CONVENTION AUTHORIZES THE APPLICATION OF THE DOMESTIC LAW OF EACH PARTY, WHICH CANNOT BE DISPUTED BY THE OTHERS OR BY AN INDIVIDUAL.

PLEASE BE ADVISED THAT THE MEXICAN CENTRAL AUTHORITY WILL NOT CONTINUE WITH THE HAGUE PROCEEDINGS FOR THE RESTITUTION OF STEPHEN IF YOUR LAWYER WILL REPRESENT YOU IN ANY PARALLEL PROCEDURE HEREAFTER.

PLEASE INFORM THIS OFFICE OF YOUR DECISION IN WRITING AS SOON AS POSSIBLE.

BROKEN TREATY

SINCERELY,
EDUARDO PEÑA HALLER,
MEXICAN CENTRAL AUTHORITY

Peña's fax message was confusing at best. Indeed I had contacted a Mexican attorney, although he had not taken any legal action. I had subsequent reports from the State Department and the Santa Clara County D.A.'s office mentioning only that another pickup attempt had been made but that Stephen and his mother were not at the home. There was no mention of a search of the house. The Mexican Central Authority told the State Department they could do no more until they could get a location on Stephen. The news was frustrating.

I had strongly warned the State Department and Mexican Central Authority that Silvia might flee with Stephen if her family became aware of the pending Mexican-generated pickup order for Stephen's return. It now appeared that Peña's office was insinuating that my retaining an attorney in Xalapa was being considered a legal action in the local family court in Xalapa and was grounds to drop my Hague petition. Bill Hilton was surprised at the position of the MCA. I expressed my intent of dismissing my Mexican attorney, David Zurutuza, but Bill insisted that I was completely within my rights. He said that the Hague Convention advocated the use of local attorneys to educate the uninformed judges so long as no parallel legal action was being sought.

In a follow up fax to the MCA, Bill Hilton cited specific Hague Convention Treaty law compelling Peña's office to refute its earlier position. I personally had a theory that Peña's office was

BROKEN TREATY

pushing back, perhaps feeling overwhelmed by the intensity of my expectations through so many channels. I had no intention of backing off. I would try every angle known and perhaps a few that no one ever thought about.

As the time since Stephen's disappearance dragged on, it became more torturous for me to see young children and their parents doing simple ordinary things together. I often wondered whether the parents appreciated what they had. Did they realize it might be taken away? I attended fewer family get-togethers, increasingly overcome with guilt about not having Stephen home yet and not anxious to describe the lack of action. The State Department wasn't helping. The Mexican Central Authority wasn't helping. Nothing was helping. It was time to do something. It was time to help myself. I decided to go to Xalapa and try to locate Stephen.

I didn't plan on doing anything foolish, I only wanted to be able to tell the Mexican authorities where he could be found. I knew that, at age 6, if Stephen was still in Xalapa, he must be in school somewhere, so I would look for him there. It was early June now and school would be letting out soon for the summer. I needed to go see what I could do in person in Xalapa. My father, Tom, and two sisters, Mary and Karen, concerned about my safety, insisted on going with me. I didn't see them as being helpful, but it made them feel as though they were doing something constructive.

In addition to the Mexican attorney I had retained to have Silvia legally served for the court in California, I had a good friend who was well respected and connected in Xalapa. He was a crucial source for information, but his identity was sensitive. He met us at the airport in Veracruz and drove us to Xalapa. I explained the developments toward Stephen's impending court action through Mexico City. My friend had been adamant about the hopelessness of any court at any level in Mexico following through with any action, but honored my pursuit.

Xalapa is nestled in the jungle highlands at a 4,000-foot elevation, ninety minutes by car from Veracruz. The city is famous for the "jalapeño" pepper and rich coffee grown there, but it is also the capital of the state of Veracruz, with a population of 350,000. The city is a state and federal governmental hub as well as home to some of Mexico's top universities. Xalapa does not attract significant tourism. Visitors are not frequent or numerous enough to avoid heavy local curiosity. Blondes or "gueros" are most conspicuous and therefore the single reason I was at all hesitant to allow my sisters to come along.

Upon arrival, I arranged a meeting with my attorney, David Zurutuza. He was frustrated that I wasn't pursuing custody in the local courts, considering a Hague Convention Treaty as nothing more than a myth. I asked him to trust me on my pursuit. I left his office with a list of schools.

My younger sister, Karen, and I pretended to be a husband and wife checking out local schools for our kids as the result of a job transfer to Xalapa. At 25 years old, Karen sported short blond hair and the fit figure of an ex-gymnast. She wore khaki pants, a polo shirt and loafers on her feet. We visited about a half dozen local private schools. We were received warmly by the staff in each school and were welcome to pop our heads into any classroom we wished to observe. I was anxious about the possibility that one of the faces I scanned on the playground or in the classroom might be Stephen's—my son that I hadn't seen in more than six months. I feared I might lose my composure and try to make a recovery right then and there.

The last school we visited was a private school on the south end of the outskirts of the city where English was the main focus. I thought it was the most likely candidate. After a brief chat with the principal, a pleasant woman in her late 40s, she invited us to have a look around before we left. Karen and I stopped at the window of each classroom and studied the students' faces. We focused on kindergarten and first grade. No sign of Stephen. We were on our way out, walking to the car, when I looked at Karen and said "Let's try something."

She gave a puzzled look, but spun around to catch up with me. We returned to the principal's office and sat again in front of the woman, this time not waiting for a gesture to sit.

"We are actually looking for my son who was brought to Xalapa six months ago by my wife. This is my sister," I came clean, while pulling out a picture of Stephen and the "wanted" poster of Silvia. I studied the principal's face for any telltale reaction.

She dropped her mouth to let out a slight gasp. I thought the reaction was strange initially, but then she slowly moved her head from side to side as she handed the photos back to me. "This boy is not a student here nor have I ever seen the mother," she slowly said. She appeared somewhat in shock, but quickly regained her composure and resumed. We thanked her for her time and headed back to the car.

"We didn't have anything to lose," offered Karen.

Stung by the failure of our search for Stephen, I only nodded. If nothing else, I could rule out where Stephen was not. I had to face the prospect that Stephen had been taken out of town.

We joined Mary and my dad back at the hotel and went out to dinner. When we returned we found a message from Zurutusa at the front desk. I reached him still in his office.

"Mr. Fenton, I received a call from your wife's attorney. She knows you are here in Xalapa and wishes to arrange a meeting between the two attorneys and a representative from the DIF," Zurutuza explained. DIF is their equivalent to our Child Protective Services.

I was hopeful that any dialogue after so long could only be a good thing. I just wanted to appeal to someone's better nature and reason that Stephen needed to come home. I had a hunch it was the principal at the last school that Karen and I visited who had tipped-off Silvia. We'd kept a pretty low profile since arriving in Xalapa, and there had been something not quite right with the woman's reaction. I wanted to demand that I see Stephen face-to-face, yet I was completely aware that I might be asked to give something in return.

"Will I be able to see my son?" I asked Zurutuza through the phone.

"I don't know. That was not discussed," he said.

The meeting was set for ten o'clock the next morning.

BROKEN TREATY

Chapter 7

The tequila sisters and a bottle of hair dye (Days missing: 185)

My dad, Mary and Karen insisted on accompanying me to the meeting at the office of Silvia's attorney. We were escorted by an office staff assistant to a well-furnished conference room where Silvia, Alberto, her attorney, a woman in her early 50s, and a dark mustached gentleman representing DIF were seated. Silvia wore a tailored skirt and jacket and had her hair pulled back, revealing a face void of expression. She and her father refused to acknowledge us or look our way. We sat and I waited silently for the first words to cross the table. After an awkward moment, Silvia's attorney spoke.

"The purpose of our visit this morning is to try and work out some kind of agreeable limited visitation for the father while the child grows up with his mother here in Xalapa," she announced in Spanish.

My father and sisters looked to me for translation at each exchange, but I didn't want to risk letting deceptions by Silvia and Alberto go unchallenged while I paused to interpret.

My response was swift and direct, "I will not be a party to any recommendations as to the visitation of my son," I began. "He has been wrongfully detained for six months from returning home to his rightful birthplace and home in the United States. Silvia does not have permission to have him here. Stephen is a U.S. born citizen and international law stipulates that he must be returned there immediately."

BROKEN TREATY

I hoped to show at once that any attempts at negotiating would be a waste of time. My dad and sisters could tell that I'd just given them all something to think about but were eager for a translation. "Silvia intends to raise Stephen here in Xalapa and they want me to agree to some visitation terms," I explained

"That's bullshit!" Karen blurted out, releasing a little gringo displeasure.

Silvia tried to capitalize on my little sister's outburst, using it as an example of American insolence.

"Now you can all see what kind of disrespectful family this is," she declared.

Mary's green eyes were wide with astonishment. She wore her blond hair short and had a slender frame. She was the closest sibling to me in age, by just under a year. She saw an opening and imposed her feelings "Silvia, you have hidden your own son from his dad for nearly half a year. How can you live with yourself?" Silvia still made no eye contact with any of us, implying no response was coming. She would only speak to the two attorneys and the DIF official.

"Stephen will be raised here in Xalapa and I know many mothers that have done the same thing with no problems," Silvia reasoned. "In California we have to eat food from a warehouse called 'Costco'; not fresh fruits and vegetables like in Mexico and there were no servants to clean or cook. It is much better for Stephen here in Xalapa."

My father sat, not offering comment. He watched to meet Alberto's eyes if he ever looked toward him; perhaps hoping to make a subliminal plea to his better judgment. But Alberto wouldn't look up. Mary and Karen had decoded Silvia's Costco comment and were starting in with a verbal counterattack. I had to try and regain a little control by calming them down before it all went to hell, sabotaging any hope to see Stephen.

"Listen carefully you guys," I warned. "I'm about to lose any chance of seeing Stephen. If you can't chill just a little, I'll have to ask you guys to wait outside the conference room." My two sisters rolled their eyes and my father sat back in his chair. I turned back to the others across the table.

"I want to see my Son now!" I demanded.

"You will see Stephen only after you drop the Hague case," Silvia asserted, her brown eyes flashing. Our eyes finally met.

"I will drop the Hague case, only after Stephen is home in California. The longer you delay the worse things are going to get for you there, Silvia!" I said firmly.

I suddenly realized that the Hague Treaty was to be leveraged in turn for being able to see Stephen. The approach was cunning but not surprising. I wondered if Alberto had finally hit the wall on his resources. Silvia turned to the DIF official and attorneys.

"I have a document from Steve giving me permission to have Stephen here in Mexico," she claimed.

"I'd like to see that document," I challenged.

She gave me a cold glance. "I don't want to show it at this time."

Knowing such a document didn't exist, I couldn't understand why she would make such a bold statement, and then refuse to show the document. I could only assume that she believed the others in the room were somewhat simple-minded.

BROKEN TREATY

Once again I made my demand. "I want to see my Son now!"

Alberto played with the clasp on his large gold Rolex.

He began to speak, still refusing eye contact.

"You continually harass our family. You have involved the California police with investigators calling my house, initiated an enormous warrant with the threat of jail for my daughter, and sent a local judge with policemen to my house," he said.

I cut him off before his next breath. "Where I come from, Alberto, they call it child abduction and it is a serious crime. I will not rest until Stephen is home where his world waits. Silvia will always be Stephen's mother; that, I will never interfere with, but she has some questions to answer back in California. You hide my son from me as though he were some kind of trophy, denying me any contact with him."

I spoke right at him, trying to catch his eyes, but he only looked away.

"I would like to see my son," I again demanded.

"Not while you continue with your Hague petition," Silvia said.

I now addressed the two attorneys and the DIF official, wagering that they might see her audacity. "I have been denied any contact with my son since last January. Until there is a diplomatic resolution to this issue, what harm would there be to a visit?" I pleaded. My attorney, who had let me speak alone until now, added a voice to the request.

"Sr. Fenton, though unwilling to seek local court remedies, still has rights as the boy's father to see his son," Zurutuza said, in a voice, a little too compromising for my comfort. Zurutuza had an uncanny resemblance to the fallen president of Panama, Manuel

BROKEN TREATY

Noriega. He was a little rough on the eyes.

The DIF official, the only one in the room with any impartial interest, now spoke up.

"I see nothing wrong with Sr. Fenton seeing his son. It's been a long time for him and I'm sure the boy would like to see his father as well," he said. The two attorneys nodded in agreement, though Silvia and her father seemed unprepared for the direction of the consensus. Under the overwhelming pressure from the attorneys and state official, Silvia realized she risked showing how sinister she was becoming.

"You can come to see him this afternoon, but you must come alone without your father and sisters," she said.

My dad and sisters had sat without any translation for over five minutes.

"They've put pressure on Silvia and Alberto to let me visit Stephen this afternoon," I related. Their eyes widened as I continued to explain. There wasn't any way to polish the restriction. They would not be allowed to see Stephen.

"Silvia says that I must be alone," I told them.

Their reaction was instantaneous. Mary's face turned pink with suppressed rage; both she and Karen stood up in protest. Karen could not control herself.

"This is the biggest load of crap I've ever seen, Silvia," she yelled. "Do you think that Steve would have ever thought about keeping you from Stephen?"

My father kept quiet. I could see the hurt in the kind gentle eyes of the former aerospace engineer while witnessing Silvia's cruelty. She was denying him any contact with one of his closest

BROKEN TREATY

grandchildren.

With the turbulence now from my sisters playing into Silvia's manipulation, I watched my chances of seeing Stephen begin to vaporize. I had to make a tough decision.

"Dad, Mary, Karen, I have to ask you to wait outside the room," I pleaded.

It was a painful request and they gave me a panicked glance, worried that I would now be vulnerable to a bad agreement. I understood their anger and hurt feelings. They were entirely justified. It pissed me off too, but I just couldn't show it now. I showed them into the adjoining waiting room then returned to the conference table. Silvia began to dictate the terms of my visit with Stephen.

"When you come to the house you cannot cry or get emotional or do anything that would upset him. You must be alone and you cannot mention California, or your family," she said. "Come at two o'clock. Don't be late."

Her face was a cold iron mask. Eyes that were once such an attractive light-coffee-brown now showed nothing more than dark pupils without borders. But I was ecstatic. I was going to see Stephen! I sat back down and we went over the details of the meeting.

Leaving the building euphoric, I herded my Dad and sisters to the rented Volkswagen and drove us all to the mall where I knew I could find a toy store. We went on a shopping spree. I was giddy with excitement. We returned to the hotel and I changed from my business suit into jeans, a blue polo shirt and tennis shoes.

My dad and sister's didn't share my enthusiasm, convinced

BROKEN TREATY

Alberto was setting up a trap to blow my head off. They would be the only ones asking questions if I disappeared.

At the heavy steel door outside the street entry to Alberto's home, I announced myself to a servant through an intercom. She could have buzzed me in, but instead I heard footsteps coming toward me through the long garden walkway. Silvia and her father opened the heavy-gauge steel door that insulated the interior from the street population. Silvia and her father were even more bitter than at the meeting.

"Remember! If you mention California, your family, or get emotional the visit will be over," Silvia said, as her father walked past me toward the street. At the sidewalk he took a few paces in either direction looking for some kind of threat. When he realized there was none, he signaled Silvia that I could pass into the garden that led to the home.

Alberto walked behind me as I moved toward the house. As we neared the front door he split off and went into the house from an entrance off the kitchen. We did not speak during our moment alone, at the big entry door, waiting until someone inside began unbolting locks. The tall, solid-wood door creaked as it slowly swung inward. I looked down to see the astonished face of the most perfect young man in the world.

My heart beat like a hammer as I dropped to my knees and put a hand on each of my Son's small shoulders. I looked into his beautiful brown eyes and said in a soft, reassuring voice, "Hello,

BROKEN TREATY

Stephen."

It was all I could do to hold back my tears. Stephen didn't say anything for a moment, needing to process what his eyes were telling him. I realized that no one had told him I was coming to see him. I held him with a long embrace, realizing he was speechless. I extended my hands cupped over his shoulders to take in his changes. He was naturally taller, but more slender than I had expected. His face was notably pale.

I took his hand as we moved to sit on the large red couch where I'd read many books to him over the years during family visits. Silvia took a chair nearby to monitor our conversation. Alberto sat with Silvia's mother at the dining room table a few yards away, watching but still unwilling to make eye contact with me. I knew he had his pistols within easy reach. I put my hatred aside, for the moment. I was only there to see Stephen.

While the moment was magical, and I glowed with pride, I was quite cognizant of the confusion in Stephen's eyes. I refrained from asking or saying anything that might jeopardize a possible second meeting. It was painful to consider that he was thinking I had abandoned him; only now deciding to drop by. It was the most difficult thing for me, unable to mention all the people and high level authorities on both sides of the border working to get him home. This was a prison visit without shatterproof glass between us. Strangely, Stephen asked no pressing questions about his situation. I considered that he, like me, saw that no good could come from awkward queries while his Mom watched and listened. I began to pull some of the gifts out of the bag.

"Stephen, I know how you love cars and I thought that you'd get

BROKEN TREATY

a kick out of this race track I found for you," I said, using English to see what language he would respond in.

"I've wanted these cars for a long time, Dad," he answered in English, with an ear-to-ear grin, still in shock at my arrival.

We sat together on the burgundy-colored carpet and began to assemble the race track. Alberto and his wife tapped ashes from their "Marlboro reds," chain smoking one after another at the dining table, annoyed that my conversation with Stephen was purely in English. I was glad to see he hadn't lost it.

At that point I really didn't care what anyone thought, so long as nobody ended my visit. Stephen talked about his Tae Kwan Do instruction. I had him show me some of his moves and did a little coaching.

Later I spoke to him in Spanish to see where he was with it. He had some basics down but preferred to converse in English. I wanted to ask questions about his school and where he was living, but Silvia was listening to everything we said.

At one point, Silvia suddenly got up and left the room. When she disappeared at the hallway, Stephen leaned toward me to whisper something, watching for his mother. Silvia reappeared only seconds later before he could disclose something, causing him to pull away.

What he intended to share would become a mystery. After two hours Silvia asked me to leave but said I could visit again the next day. I was to call in the morning for a specific time. I tried to reassure Stephen that the absurdity of the situation must come to an end, the only way I could—with a comforting look from my eyes and stout hugs. I left Alberto's home, with the understanding that we'd visit again tomorrow.

BROKEN TREATY

I shared the details of my visit with my Dad and sisters. They were happy to see the hope in my face, but even happier that I was okay. The bitterness, though, about being denied a visit with Stephen limited their enthusiasm.

The next morning when I called the house as instructed, no one answered. I called all afternoon with the same results. Finally, at 5:00 p.m., I went to the house and was met at the steel door by Silvia's brother, Alberto Jr. He said that because of my refusal to drop my Hague Convention petition, Silvia had decided to flee with Stephen. He told me that he didn't know where she was. I sat on the ground and put my head in my hands, realizing that Silvia had retreated back into hiding with Stephen. Alberto Jr. closed the large steel door. Silvia and Stephen could be halfway to Mexico City by now.

We could have stayed another day or two but there was no use in remaining. My attorney, Zurutuza, again recommended filing a motion in the local family court to flush Silvia out but I knew it would cost me the Hague petition. He further advised me that the DIF would not get involved unless I was willing to take legal action locally, again jeopardizing the Hague case.

We arranged to fly home to California the next day. The flight was somber. We all realized there was no easy answer to bringing Stephen home. Mary and Karen were furious about the tease of seeing Stephen, but I saw how it was affecting my dad. The white-haired WWII veteran pilot should have been bouncing grandchildren on his lap rather than helplessly watching his grandson become an international abduction subject. While every grandchild was equally loved, Stephen had grown especially close to both my father

BROKEN TREATY

and mother as they had often helped in caring for him after Silvia and I separated.

After learning the fate of my second promised visit at the house, Mary and Karen found a liquor store near the hotel and brought a bottle of tequila to their room on our last night. While finishing off the bottle, they got into some cheap black hair dye they had brought on the trip to go incognito if they felt circumstances warranted a disguise.

Now, midflight on the five-hour plane ride, I realized how hung over the two were and noticed what they had done to their hair. The black didn't stop at the hair. They had carelessly stained their faces with some of the dye, looking like derelicts who'd been dumpster diving at an ink-toner factory. I loved my sisters for making the trip, but took a seat away from them while they tried to ease their condition by consuming "resort drinks" on a plane, only to offer more colorful cynicism. If not for the impending complexities ahead for bringing Stephen home, I would have found humor in my sisters' behavior.

I wouldn't stop until I had my son home again, but I was beginning to question whether I was on the right path.

BROKEN TREATY

Chapter 8

A discreet note

The day after returning from Mexico, I briefed Bill Hilton on events. I hadn't mentioned the trip beforehand knowing that the State Department would not approve. Bill though, was pleased to pass on the information of my findings and felt as though we had been able to flush Silvia out. The fact that she now had an attorney indicated, that she might be taking a legal position and be forced to declare a location. Hilton was adamant about staying out of any local Xalapa litigation and let the Hague solution take its course. The problem I had with that was that if Alberto saw his options disappearing he might do something drastic like send Silvia and Stephen off to Mexico City, which he may have done alreay.

I reported my findings to all involved in the case, including The State Department, VCA, and The National Center for Missing and Exploited Children. After I had given Melanie Headrick details of the trip to Xalapa, she asked if I had heard about Dave's rescue. Dave was the father of a young boy who had been taken by his mother to an island in the Dutch West Indies. I had met Dave in parental support meetings hosted by the VCA. According to Melanie, Dave and some close friends recovered his Son from his mother's car. They boxed the mother's car in on a quite island road at night. After pulling his son out a broken window, Dave and one other person took his son and fled by boat to a neighboring island, also a different country. Dave was apprehended as he and his son stepped onto the dock of the next island, but was released when he proved that he had full custody of his son. David's two friends were apprehended, arrested and convicted; each serving one year in prison for their part. I was ecstatic for Dave's reunion with his young son but sensitive to what the boy must have witnessed.

I was able to see Dave at the next VCA meeting. He brought his son. I marveled at the little 3 year old entertaining himself on the floor underfoot as Dave shared details about the rescue. He recalled the many times his wife had hung up on him while she was concealing their son. Now that he had recovered his son, his wife continued to hang up on him even though she had initiated the call. She wasn't willing to return and re-establish contact with her son, fearing prosecution.

I admired Dave and understood the motivating force behind his action. I also felt for his son, for what he'd endured, and for the current isolation from his mother.

In July I learned that the MCA in Mexico City was preparing new orders to be executed by the Family Court in Xalapa. Still, I saw July come and go with no results, knowing that August offered little hope when the Mexican government shuts down for vacation. I was told that a new pickup order would be ready in early September.

The September order was issued and the authorities went to Alberto's home. They now had permission to break down the door and do a complete search. However the family, after explaining that they did not know Stephen or Silvia's whereabouts, countered with orders from another Judge who had awarded custody to Silvia, but who had no knowledge of the Hague proceedings. Silvia's custody order would be subsequently revoked by the terms of the Hague Treaty as any subsequent custody orders are invalidated automatically, but the process would take four to six weeks. There could now be no recovery possible until November. I was growing concerned.

Around this time I had been fortunate enough to get some attention with my case at the State Department through California Senator Dianne Feinstein's office in Washington. My sister Mary's in-laws had connections, and they enlisted the help of Feinstein's office to look into the delays from Mexico. By this time, the only reason I had contact with our State Department was to share information about my son's case. The probing by Feinstein's staff seemed to hit a nerve with the caseworkers and communication was strained after that.

My desperation grew each day and wavered from hopefulness to panic. There was just enough hope sprinkled on occasion that it kept me from doing something dramatic, but I was not opposed to anything that might get results. On an impulse, I researched a bilingual local private investigator who claimed to have countless legitimate contacts in Mexico. All I wanted from him was to know if he could learn Stephen's whereabouts so that I could pass that information on to the MCA. I gave him a $500 cash down payment only to never hear from him. I traced him to an address after a couple weeks of non-returned calls. He answered the door in the afternoon wearing a bathrobe, offended that I had come to his home. He became apprehensive and said that his contacts had turned up nothing but would call when he heard something.

BROKEN TREATY

Considering all the money I'd poured into the regular channels, the money wasted on the private investigator was a cheap lesson. Beyond the financial pain, what disturbed me more was that someone would capitalize so boldly from another's grief.

Waiting for action on the part of the Mexican Central Authority was like watching grass grow. In late October, I learned that the authorities in Xalapa had acquired permission to break down the steel entry door regardless of any new custody orders that the family might present and search the premises. This would be the fourth pickup attempt. I considered the news encouraging but I reserved judgment. Two days later I learned that the attempt to execute the pick-up was frustrated by a new order on Silvia's part claiming that her constitutional rights were being violated. The order was called an "amparo"—a Mexican federal injunction that temporarily disabled the Hague petition.

I operated these days in a constant state of numbness, somehow finding the strength each day to get out of bed in the morning and walk past Stephen's room. Then I'd spend another day contemplating how I was going to bring him home. The costs of the legal process were devastating, but I somehow believed that money created enough influence in the right direction to create opportunities.

Although not completely understanding my own reasons, I began squirreling away any surplus of cash that was left over after my legal expenses. All the documents had been filed and attorneys could do no more here or abroad; so, I was able to put some cash into a private emergency fund.

Only a few days after the last pickup attempt, I attended a missing children media event, where in private I was handed a note with a name and phone number scribbled on it by an official with specific knowledge regarding my case. The official said that any connection was to be strictly anonymous. Given the source, there was little to be skeptical about. The alarming part was that it put the hopelessness of my case in perspective.

On a sunny morning in early November, I met with Patrick M. Buckman at the home of my parents, Tom and Hilda Fenton, in Los Altos. My Dad is a retired aerospace engineer and my mother was teaching court stenography to adult students. Both parents were in their 70s.

Pat was tall, with dark features; and he has a resonance in his voice that commands attention. I knew only that after a career as a police detective he started a private investigation firm. He fell into a couple of difficult child recovery cases and soon found himself as the go-to guy for frustrated, left-behind parents. He was well known for finding and bringing kids home safe from all over the world, although I was unaware of his prominence at the time.

"The first thing I need to ask is if you have a custody order?" Pat asked.

"Yes. I have a copy if you'd like to see it now?" I replied.

"Good, because otherwise, I wouldn't be able to help you," he replied. "Our group does not use weapons of any kind and we keep the safety of the child foremost in any recovery. Are there any weapons in the home where you believe your son might be?" Buckman asked.

"Yes, my wife's father has a collection of handguns. A 9 mm pistol is his favorite."

"Then any rescue would have to be away from the home, maybe on Stephen's way to or at school. Do you know his daily routine or where he goes to school?" he asked.

This was a difficult question. I felt ashamed that I could not tell him exactly where Stephen was; only seeing him for two short hours five months ago.

"I have no current information on his location. The family at the house only tells me they don't know where he is. I do believe he is in Xalapa, maybe at another home," I said.

There was an awkward silence around the table after my painful admission. Pat broke it at last.

"I could go down there and do some surveillance, but it might be a big waste of money if we had no idea where to look for him," he suggested.

I began to have confidence in this man, seeing that he didn't want to spend our money without reliable information on where to look for Stephen.

"If we had that information what do you think the rescue would cost?" my father asked.

"Only guessing, off the top of my head I would say somewhere around $30,000, including a surveillance trip to establish his location," he said.

The figure to me was staggering. It might as well have been $30 million.

Buckman took copious notes as we spoke. I had a map of southern Mexico and had tried to get my hands on some aeronautical charts of the region but had no luck. I was told that they were hard to come by because drug smugglers found them so valuable. I mentioned a small airfield along the highway from Veracruz to Xalapa about fifteen minutes out of town. As a former student pilot, I thought how great it would be to fly Silvia and Stephen in our own small plane to Xalapa for visits when we wished, which drew my interest to the airfield. Pat took particular interest in this information, asking me for a rough location.

I explained my frustration with the State Department and the Mexican Central Authority and all the attempts to bring Stephen home through legal channels. He nodded.

"The Hague Treaty is a great idea but a lot of things need to be ironed out before it's going to be minimally effective to bring kids home from Mexico. I've never personally heard of a child recovered from Mexico through the Hague Treaty," he admitted.

I sat quietly, thinking about the significance of what he'd just disclosed.

"How do you think your son will react when you tell him you're taking him home?" he asked.

It was a fair question, although I hadn't really thought about it.

"Pat, when this all started, Stephen cried over the phone to come get him. Hell, I don't think he will be anything but annoyed with me for taking so long. I can't imagine there would be any kind of an issue," I said.

"Something you should know is that kids easily adapt to new situations. It's just part of their survival mechanism to adjust and leave the past behind. The longer a child remains missing the more likely he will resist recovery," he paused. "It could mean the difference between a long overdue reunion and getting thrown in a Mexican prison."

BROKEN TREATY

Buckman's comments were sobering. He raised questions that I hadn't wanted to consider, though nothing would deter me. Buckman only reaffirmed my fear about time being such a critical component. Buckman's insight only reinforced the need to get a location on Stephen. Without a location or even where to look, all was irrelevant.

Money was a factor, too. I hadn't corralled that kind of cash although I was working seven days a week. For the moment I could only reinvest in new hope that a Hague Treaty resolution was imminent.

We thanked Pat for his time and promised to keep him abreast of developments. I felt that the guy was honest and had integrity, leaving me with a good feeling. Buckman asked that I only talk about details on a land line. He wouldn't discuss specifics over a cell phone and I spoke to no one about our meeting.

After the failure of the latest pickup attempt I decided to make an official request seeing that a recovery was not likely before the end of the year. I wanted to see Stephen during the holidays, with the blessing of some official entity on the Mexican side. The U.S. State Department was now no longer helpful. I suspected that they knew the probable outcome, but would let time soften the impact. I never expected any direct results from Washington, but felt deceived that they weren't honest about what I should expect.

As Thanksgiving approached the possibility of passing Christmas alone became more and more likely. As the anniversary of Stephen's quiet abduction to Mexico approached, I saw less inclination to sit tight. I would go to Mexico and put my face in front of the Mexican Central Authority staff and plead my case. I would show them that

BROKEN TREATY

I am just a father trying to bring his son home. While Washington and Mexico were still talking about the probability of Stephen being returned before Christmas, I just couldn't hand over my soul to another parade of empty promises. I had nothing to lose and perhaps I could achieve something.

I knew that there would be a cold initial reception by the MCA; it was unlikely that they had ever come face to face with an American parent. There were no guarantees that they would even see me and I had already been told by our State Department to "not even think about going." One thing I had on my side was that I had a good knowledge of Mexican culture and a good command of the language.

Thus on Thanksgiving Day, as a Mexicana DC-10 punched through a dark morning sky on a five-hour flight to Mexico City, I thought about what I would say if I could get the staff at the MCA in Mexico City to see me.

My thoughts jumped ahead, to the moment that I could say: "It's time to go home Son."

BROKEN TREATY

BROKEN TREATY

Chapter 9

Thanksgiving in Mexico City

It is said that Mexico City has the highest level of air pollution in the world. The "punch-in-the-nose" aroma of burned diesel fuel filled the air as I meandered out of the airport. I looked for one of the back-street illegal taxis. I always saved a few pesos using the illegal taxies, though I knew a woman who had been robbed at gunpoint with her mother by one of these taxistas. I'm no fan of large cities, but Mexico City struck me as a friendlier place. Like other cities, it has everything to offer, but the locals are courteous and eager to please if you are courteous and respectful.

I found a hotel within walking distance of the federal building where the MCA office was located. It was now eight o'clock in the morning. I was still unsure if I would be seen by anyone, but I had two full days of nowhere else to be. I wasn't sure what I would say, but believed instinct would be my guide. I knew to be respectful, well aware that a bad attitude or arrogance would make my file hard to find. Along with my documents, I had a Wilbur Smith novel to signal that I had plenty of time – if they believed I'd grow impatient and leave.

In front of the grey stone building that was home to Mexico's Foreign Ministry, I looked up at the building's 20 stories and it reminded me of the first day I met with Melanie Headrick at the district attorney's offices in San Jose.

"Mexican courtesy with gringo charm," I said to myself.

The security guard in the lobby called up and announced my

BROKEN TREATY

arrival to the MCA office and then I sat for a good hour watching the guard watch me. I was dressed in a grey striped business suit. I knew I only had one shot at this with the Mexican Central Authority and wanted to demonstrate to the MCA that they were dealing with a father who at least cared enough to appear presentable.

A bell rang below at the guard station. "Te esperan arriba,"—"They are waiting for you above," the security officer said, as he guided me to an elevator; the only other door on this floor. The elevator took me to the top of the building where I was met by another security guard and escorted through another secured door.

I walked in on a typical office atmosphere with secretaries tapping away at keyboards. The keyboards grew silent as I became noticed and whispers replaced the noise of office machines. I felt a slight uneasiness in the air as though something important was about to happen.

A woman approached me extending her hand to introduce herself.

"Yo soy Laura Duclaud," she said. I responded in Spanish introducing myself.

Laura looked young, maybe 25 years old. She had fine, almost black shoulder-length hair and a pleasant magazine-cover smile.

"Mr. Fenton, you should realize that our agency has strict policies against meeting with parents pending the return of their children," she said.

Before I could say something inventive, she continued.

"...but Sr. Peña and the entire staff are very familiar with your case and we can give you a few minutes to go over the status if you would like," she offered.

BROKEN TREATY

Before responding, I studied her eyes, probing for signs. I thought I detected that this case was important to her, yet complicated and troubling. We had spent hours on the phone over dozens of calls, but, through her clinical demeanor, I detected a personal interest.

"Srta. Duclaud, I need to find out what's going on with my son's case. I'd really appreciate any time you and Sr. Peña could take," I replied.

She asked me to have a seat while we waited for Peña. Already this was going much further than I had anticipated. I'd wanted an audience to plead my case and I was getting it! Invariably, any services from officials required a contribution. Even the documents for permission as a foreigner to marry Silvia required special compensation to a select individual. In my briefcase I had an envelope containing $1,000. There is protocol to making an offer. The wrong words or poor timing could be offensive.

As I was introduced to some of the staff, I saw that no one seemed over 30 years old, some maybe just out of college.

Eduardo Peña walked toward me and introduced himself. Confident in stride with a firm handshake, he sported a well groomed mustache, was surprisingly tall and about my age. Peña motioned me toward a seating area with comfortable sofas and armchairs arranged in a rectangular pattern so that we all faced each other. I sat alone in the middle of a large sofa now facing Peña, Duclaud, and two other staff members.

With all previous contacts over the phone, I had spoken Spanish, and they seemed to appreciate and prefer it. Here face to face I let intuition kick in and waited to see which language they would use to open dialogue with.

BROKEN TREATY

In a seasoned diplomatic tone Peña began. He spoke in perfect English.

"Mr. Fenton I realize that it has been a difficult time during the absence of your son, now nearly a year. Rest assured that we are doing everything in our power to see the rightful return of your son to his home in California. Your wife has been extremely elusive in our efforts to recover the boy from the home you indicated. It would appear that your son's grandfather in Xalapa has gone to great lengths to circumvent the federal court orders from here in Mexico City while claiming not to know the whereabouts of your son and wife," he said.

I was getting the impression that my case was becoming a black eye to the MCA and they were becoming frustrated.

"Mr. Peña, I am aware of the earnest efforts of your staff to see to the return of my son. Every day that passes is another day I will have missed in my son's life," I calmly explained.

"I want to know if you believe that there is a chance that he could be home by Christmas, and if not, is there any way that your office could arrange for me to visit my son over the holidays without jeopardizing the Hague petition process?" I asked.

Laura Duclaud and the two other staffers watched Peña's face to see how he would respond.

"Mr. Fenton, we believe that your son will be back with you in California before Christmas and that there will be no need for an arranged visit with your son. A new pickup order is being processed at this moment and a judge and policeman will be sent to the home with the order overruling her local custody order. They have authority to break down the door to the home," he said.

BROKEN TREATY

I wasn't ready to get excited. If this department still didn't have a location on Stephen what good would a new pickup order be?

I took a moment to open up the large file I carried with me. Inside I had a copy of every postal and fax correspondence sent and received about my case. I leafed through those until I located a separate file containing photos of Stephen. I handed the photos to the woman nearest me and I sat silently for a moment. As the photos slowly circulated through the staff members I saw their reaction as they remarked on how striking they thought Stephen was. When the photos reached Laura Duclaud, I sensed again a personal interest as she studied the intricate features of Stephen's young face. I wanted her to think about Stephen often.

Peña seemed disinterested though and handed the photos back to me. "I would like a moment alone with Mr. Fenton, please," Peña instructed in Spanish. I thought about the envelope with 10 one-hundred dollar bills in my briefcase. But there was a small flag. Peña had worn through the soles of his dress shoes. He was in a powerful position as head of the Mexican Central Authority division of the Ministry of Exterior Relations. Although commanding a great deal of clout the position doesn't pay much. It occurred to me that Peña might be a maverick with scruples – offering a level of dignity to the department. I refrained from probing dialogue.

As soon as we were alone the atmosphere changed. Peña was direct.

"Mr. Fenton, do you realize that you have put your Hague petition in jeopardy by hiring an attorney in Xalapa? Those are grounds to dismiss the case according to the treaty," he said.

Courtesies were abandoned. The gloves had come off – the fight was all about Stephen now. I got in Peña's face.

BROKEN TREATY

"Do you really think I would do anything to put my Hague case at risk, Sr. Peña? The attorney, Mr. Zurutusa in Xalapa, was hired only as an agent for information and to have my wife legally served with due process as required by law in California. He was instructed to completely avoid the courts and any litigation. My attorney, Bill Hilton, whom you know very well, knows the Hague Convention Treaty better than anyone else alive and sanctioned the use of Zurutusa's limited services. I have done nothing outside the terms of the treaty."

Peña had taken a shot at me with bad information and I had caught him up. Not bothering to respond to my remarks he quickly changed subjects and softened his demeanor. My bark bared more fang than I intended, but seemed to get his attention.

"Mr. Fenton, I realize that you are intent on seeing your son returned to you but you must let the legal process take its course. It is only a matter of time before your wife will run out of options and will have to hand over your son to the authorities for his return to California." he paused, gazing momentarily at the floor. I took advantage of the moment.

"How do you expect to recover my son when no one seems to have a location on him?" I asked in a direct firm tone. He resumed eye contact, remembering he was a diplomat.

"We here have dealt with anxious parents who become impatient with the process and try to take matters into their own hands. They may actually try to recover their children themselves. In this scenario, three things can happen: One, if you are caught you face prison. Two, you will probably have your Hague case dismissed. Three, you may anger any judges presiding over similar cases here in Mexico and jeopardize the potential recovery for another parent. Mr. Fenton, do I make myself clear?"

"Yes, Mr. Peña, I just want my son back. He cried over the phone with me, pleading to bring him home when I still had contact with him. I promised I would and I don't intend to let him down. It's a promise I intend to keep," I said.

"Go home, Mr. Fenton, with the assurance that the Mexican Central Authority will get your son home soon," Peña said.

Out of all the corrupt officials in Mexico, when I needed one the most, I was dealing with a young scrupulous staff. The flip side was that if I couldn't get cooperation in the usual way, maybe Alberto couldn't either. Maybe we were on a level playing field, but I couldn't forget the two most important laws in Mexico: Power and money.

My visit with the Central Mexican Authority was over. I had no idea what if any impression I'd left the staff with. Maybe at the least they would push for results to make me go away.

Having completely forgotten about today being Thanksgiving, I noticed restaurants displaying Thanksgiving menus outside for the tourists and a significant American population in the city.

I took a nap back at the hotel and traded my suit for some jeans and a comfortable sweater and had a taxi take me somewhere "quiet and dark." Tonight I would drink some good tequila and perhaps escape. I ended up in the "Zona Rosa," a high-density night club, restaurant and bar neighborhood, popular with both tourists and wealthier locals.

I found an obscure out of the way bar that no tourist had likely ever seen and grabbed a seat at a small table inside. The place was dark, quiet and nearly empty. A shot of "Heradura Gold" was set in front of me. A woman soon approached my table and struck up a conversation in Spanish.

"I overheard you speaking Spanish to the bartender. Would you mind if I sat with you?"

"Of course not, have a seat." She called herself "Lolita." She had long dark hair that was pony-tailed off to one side and lay across the front of one shoulder. A black leather skirt wrapped her thighs and a sleeveless red blouse that wasn't inappropriate for the mild and still-early evening. She had a contagious smile. I knew what would be coming.

It was refreshing to talk with someone having no knowledge of my misery. She asked me to buy her a brandy with coke.

"But with no ice, right?" I asked. A smile was her answer.

We talked small talk about Mexico City, my years at college in Puebla, only an-hour-and-a-half southeast of the city, and about life in the United States. She'd never been, but she wanted to take her daughter some day, if she could ever save enough money. She looked away from me, as though taking inventory of the room, then re-engaged her eyes with mine.

"Would you like to take me home tonight?" she casually asked.

"Actually no, but I'd be happy to buy you another drink if you'd like to talk a little more," I replied.

She wasn't offended. This was how she made a living and I was gentle about passing judgment on anyone with enough ambition to chase a living. Our conversation resumed comfortably. She'd taken a liking to me and confessed that she'd never talked to an American before. She'd seen the way Americans treat the Mexicans here in their own country and found them appalling for the most part. I didn't try to make any excuses for them, I only mentioned a disease called the "Ugly American Syndrome" and she began to laugh.

She had questions by-the-tubful and before long had extracted the reason I'd come to Mexico City. The details became more disturbing as she considered them, commenting that she'd known women who'd left their husbands in the U.S., taking the kids back to Mexico knowing the husbands won't follow; not wanting to give up life in the U.S., but also aware that the courts typically award custody to the mother in Mexico. She took more interest in my problem than I intended, now searching my eyes.

"If you want your son back, you will have to go to Xalapa and take him home to California yourself. If you think the officials in our government are going to help to you, you are very foolish. They will make promises until you give up and stop bothering them," she warned.

It struck me that I'd heard a similar lecture in English. I thought about Georgia Hilgeman at the VCA, nearly 2,000 miles away back in California and how these two women, both from such polarized backgrounds were so similarly adamant about the only hope of getting my son out.

"The judges here resent the way your country tries to push Mexico around. When they see a political opportunity to retaliate against the United States, they will," she warned.

I needed to leave the bar. I had unintentionally monopolized the time of the only female in the place as stony glares from surrounding tables stabbed at my tequila armour. I said goodbye to the insightful hooker and mother. She made a last ditch effort to strike a deal. I only smiled and shook her hand, passing a folded fifty dollar bill, and made my way outside to catch a taxi back to the hotel.

I found an earlier flight back home to California the next morning since there was nothing more I could do in Mexico City. I had weak moments of considering a rental car and driving to Xalapa to try to see Stephen, or at least confront the family and plead to see him. The warnings had been fervent, though, and I had to weigh once again the chances of jeopardizing the Hague solution against being turned away from seeing Stephen.

I boarded the flight back to San Francisco reassuring myself that the trip had been the right thing to do. I could only wait to see. Even false hope was still hope at this point, with no better direction.

The following Monday morning back home, I gave a synopsis of my meeting with Peña and his staff to my attorney Bill Hilton. He said my meeting might help, but that the U.S. State Department had learned about my visit to Mexico City and had already expressed displeasure.

I once worked with a guy who was a reluctant soldier in Vietnam. He told me about soldiers becoming so desperately bored; stuck in the jungle during the war, that every now and then a soldier would discreetly toss a grenade with the pin still in it into a tent full of officers working a big battle board. There was no explosion, but one got to see a lot of important people move really fast.

There was no threat that I would explode, but hoped that I had somehow created a sense of urgency with the MCA for my son's return.

Chapter 10

The Vague Convention Treaty

On my return to California, I continued hoping that something would pop. I shared the details of my trip with Melanie Headrick, Bill Hilton, Senator Diane Feinstein's office, the VCA, and anyone who might still be interested at the State Department. Naturally, the State Department wasn't pleased. I think that the only reliable diplomatic policy regarding left-behind parents was the "verbal spanking policy" that surfaced anytime protocol was not observed or that parents took a proactive position.

I kept up with calls and correspondence by fax to the MCA, anticipating a new pickup attempt for Stephen at the Xalapa house again, with permission to break the door down if needed for a search of the house. The last week in November saw no new action toward a recovery handed down from Mexico City to the family court in Xalapa.

As December came around I started to get some encouraging reports from Peña's office. The family court judge in Xalapa was ready to issue a new pickup order. I was advised that Laura Duclaud, the woman at the MCA who seemed to take a personal interest in Stephen's return, was asked to come to Xalapa at which time the judge would issue the pickup order turning Stephen over to Duclaud for the trip to Mexico City.

I was cynical but there was nothing to lose, half believing that Silvia and Alberto were backed into a corner. When my father shared the news of the impending recovery with the rest of the family, my

BROKEN TREATY

sisters Mary and Karen came over to prepare Stephen's room for his return. I hadn't been able to spend much time in his room. Seeing his toys and clothes, a pair of shoes tossed on the closet floor was much too painful. Walking past his closed door every morning was a constant reminder that I'd failed for so long.

My dynamo sisters, leaping toward the task at hand, thrust the door open, pulled up his blinds, and allowed sunlight to chase away the darkness. I followed the girls in and drew a little inspiration from their uncanny ability to find humor in any situation. They immediately peeled off blankets and sheets from the unmade bed.

"I'm not really into washing bedding," Mary quipped as she brushed by me with an armload headed for the washer. "I usually just turn the sheets over every six months and my kids don't know the difference."

"I'm going to marry a guy so damn rich that I won't have to wash bedding, I'll just toss out the old bedding and open new packages from the store," Karen joked.

"Steve, you realize that Stephen won't fit into any of his clothes," Mary said, sorting through one of the dresser drawers. "You're going to have a lot of shopping to do. Should we clear out his old things?"

"No, leave everything in the drawers. He'll probably only have the clothes on his back and there may still be a few things that fit him," I answered. It was difficult to speculate that he'd kept growing without me.

While the girls buzzed about getting his room shipshape, I took a moment to study the undisturbed toys that crowded his dresser, desk and shelves. His favorite picture books and beginning readers next to the bed caught my eye. He loved to listen to me read the advanced books that were a challenge to him as I lay down next to him before lights out.

Mary and Karen finished what they had come to do and were off again on their next adventure. They parted with heartfelt hugs, saying if Stephen wasn't home soon they would send me a "cleaning bill."

I sat on the edge of his freshly made bed and studied the things in his room. I looked over the half-finished model submarine we had worked on together, his display of Lego creations left as he had built them, and sorted through some of his vast baseball card collection. On a shelf stood a portrait of Stephen riding a mock killer whale with my sister Mary and her husband, Jeff. They had recently married and asked if they could take Stephen to Marine World for the day when the photo was taken.

Jeff, my brother-in-law, had attended Brown University and, as luck would have it, wound up rooming with John F. Kennedy Jr. The two men remained close after college and Jeff asked Kennedy to be a groomsman in his wedding to Mary. Silvia and I attended a rehearsal dinner at the home of Jeff's parents in San Mateo, California, the night before the wedding, taking 3-year-old Stephen. Later in the evening, noticing that Stephen was no longer at my side, I went searching for him. I found him curled up in Kennedy's lap on a large white sofa, trying to take a nap. Kennedy was very polite and insisted that Stephen was not a problem. It would be a fun story to share when my son was old enough to know whose lap he had crawled into. The image was as vivid as the night it happened.

Sitting in his room gave me hope. The depression would have

been overwhelming if the possibility of recovery hadn't looked so promising.

I had begun checking out flight availability to Mexico City on a daily basis, anticipating a call from Melanie Headrick saying Stephen had been taken into protective custody by Mexican officials. They were to take him to Mexico City and turn him over to Melanie for the flight back to San Francisco. I would not be welcome, but would make arrangements to be in Mexico City nonetheless. Melanie had a rough kindness, but deep disdain for abducting parents. She had flown all over the United States and to several countries to recover stolen children. I knew she would be the next best thing until I could hold Stephen again.

On Wednesday, December 8, 1993, I received word from Peña's office that the day before, the family court judge in Xalapa had executed a pickup order once again at Alberto's house, but that no one would come to the door. Peña said the judge was preparing paperwork that would allow the police to break down the door to search the home and interrogate everyone for information on Stephen's whereabouts if he wasn't found inside. I became concerned about the potential psychological effects on Stephen while I couldn't be there.

On Thursday, December 9th, Peña's office informed me that the forced entry order would be executed that day or the next and told me to call back Friday. When I called Mexico Friday afternoon, I learned that the latest pickup order had been thwarted by new documents that Alberto presented to the authorities at the home. Allegedly from a "superior authority," the documents invoked an "amparo," a type of federal injunction, addressing claims that

BROKEN TREATY

Silvia's constitutional rights were being violated and that she had been granted custody of Stephen by the local family court.

The amparo is a Mexican legal procedure from 1847 designed to protect any Mexican citizen believing that their constitutional rights are being violated by a Mexican authority. The amparo renders a Hague Convention petition useless, often tying up the issue in federal court for months or years. Multiple appeals may also be filed. In Mexico, the Hague Convention Treaty becomes the "Vague" Convention Treaty. It is unclear to many why the U.S. pursued Mexico as a reciprocal signatory partner to the Hague Treaty in the first place.

Naturally, the news was devastating. I was becoming numb, not knowing where to go from here. Peña's office assured me that his people were preparing a very aggressive challenge to these new orders Silvia had obtained. The only problem was that these new orders were difficult to trace to a source. It appeared that these documents were approved, stamped and then buried with no access. No one could produce a copy to Peña's office. Only Silvia's family and her attorney had copies and were not making them accessible.

The following week I learned that the courts in Mexico would be closing down until sometime in January. I called Peña's office on the outside chance that I might get to see Stephen during the Christmas holidays through a court-sanctioned visit. Laura Duclaud informed me that the family court in Xalapa had not been cooperative and that the MCA would aggressively pursue the case after the beginning of the year. I had to prepare for a rough time through the holidays. This would mark a year now since Stephen was taken to Mexico. The holidays would never be the same.

BROKEN TREATY

I spent the next day shopping for gifts for my son that he'd probably never see. I would send them express to Alberto's home, holding out a small hope that someone would accept the package and get them to Stephen, wherever he was. I knew that when I would ask for Stephen on Christmas I would be met with a dial tone.

I spent Christmas Eve at my parents' home. The liquor was plentiful and numbed a little of my anguish. I had wanted to avoid the scenario, the wondrous excitement of my siblings' small children tearing open gifts, but my mom had pleaded with me to be there. She didn't want me alone on Christmas.

A call to Xalapa that night and a subsequent call Christmas Day produced what I expected; no response, only the "click" of a phone receiver dropped back into its cradle. In a moving moment during a gift exchange, Karen, my youngest sister, handed me an envelope with a bank statement in it – a trust account showing a fifty dollar deposit in Stephen's name. She explained that the money was to be devoted to the rescue. In that moment I realized that my Dad had shared details of our private meeting with Buckman. I lost it for the first time. I began to quietly cry and left the room.

Christmas was rough and New Years wasn't any better. Another attempt to reach Stephen had once again been cut off. I was anxious to see the holidays behind me so I could get back to making as much money as possible for whatever lay ahead.

I was waiting when the Mexican court system resumed business in the middle of January. Peña's office again began making noise about having the previous orders rescinded and generating new pickup orders. I was all for their efforts, but now I believed that anything short of a Vatican emissary knocking on Alberto's door

BROKEN TREATY

offered no promise.

I realized that I hadn't been in touch with my contact back in Xalapa for over a month, nor had I called to wish him the best over the holidays. On a Monday night, January 17, I called my friend in Xalapa. The information he had was pivotal.

"Steve, this is a good thing that you called. I was going to call you tomorrow when the rates aren't so expensive." I sensed the seriousness in his voice.

"Listen carefully. Your son is living at Alberto's house with his mother. A close friend of my sister stopped to buy some tortillas at the tortilleria next to Alberto's house when Silvia and Stephen drove up and into the garage. My sister's friend was able to see the sweater that your son was wearing through the car window. We are pretty sure it is part of the uniform for the private school you thought he might be attending, Las Hayas, when you came with your sisters and your father in June."

My heart raced. This time with excitement not panic.

"My friend, you have no idea how important this information is. Is there any other news?" I asked.

"Yes, I heard from your attorney David Zurutuza, that your wife actually went to see the governor's wife for help and was turned away. He also says that Silvia has been seen going out with one of the family court judges who has been involved in the case," he said.

"Steve, this is all I can tell you at this time. If I learn anything else I'll let you know right away. Good luck," he said. Our call ended.

A theoretical alignment was establishing itself. It was time to make contact with Buckman. I reserved any excitement, taking into

BROKEN TREATY

account the initial rough costs, and whether he would even consider taking my case.

Chapter 11

Time to do something

I met with Pat Buckman in my parents' home a few days after getting the information from my contact about Stephen's location. This time I was armed with a city map of Xalapa showing the street to Alberto's house and the school on the outskirts of the city.

After some effort, I found old charts showing the location, elevation and runway length at El Lencero, a small air field situated just south of Xalapa along the only highway running south toward Veracruz. The field had a tower which meant interaction with field authorities. I was encouraged that Buckman saw the same strategic value in the field as I did. The closer we studied the concept, the more sense it made.

"Brownsville is the closest U.S. port of entry. Would that be our destination?" I probed.

Judging by his forthright response; he seemed to have already considered that.

"We'd fly out heading due south into Guatemala. You would then catch a commercial flight from Guatemala City with your son back to the U.S."

Flying into Guatemala was a variable in the formula that I didn't want to test.

"I'm a little worried that I might get into a custody squabble between the U.S. and Mexico after arriving in Guatemala. Why can't we simply fly directly back to the States in the small plane?"

"I don't think that the plane we have access to has the range to make it back without refueling. And believe me, we don't want to have to land again in Mexico and risk getting detained, after the authorities began sorting things out," he paused, then added, "I'll need to go down to Xalapa and do some surveillance and get their daily routine down. I will be down there several days, and I'll need $5,000 for travel and expenses in advance."

The table became silent. Buckman had laid his cards down for me to see. Now it was time to put up or shut up. I couldn't help but think about the money I'd given to the other private investigator—without even a phone call back. Buckman made no promises but his moves gave me confidence that a rescue was feasible. He seemed comforted with my intimate understanding of the family and the layout of the city.

"I'll have a cashier's check to you tomorrow," I said.

The moment was a profound turning point in my endeavor. For the first time since Stephen's disappearance, I finally was pursuing my early instincts that a rescue would be the only real chance.

Two weeks later, while Buckman was in Xalapa gathering information and trying to verify Stephen's location, I was standing in line at a supermarket check-out on my way home from work. Some bold letters on a headline in a weekly woman's magazine caught my eye. The front cover mentioned the story of a private investigator who specialized in finding and returning missing children from all over the world. I opened it up to see Buckman's picture splattered across two pages, accompanied by an article describing some of his most colorful cases. After reading the article, I found a website featuring a profile on him.

Patrick M. Buckman started Buckman & Associates in San Francisco in 1967. He worked with firms, families and individuals on a worldwide scale. Over the years, he had recovered millions of dollars hidden all over the globe. He had located corporate executives charged with selling high-tech secrets and also provided security for the wealthy and famous. It was clear that he was one of the country's top investigators.

Born in San Francisco, Buckman enlisted in the Air Force at an early age and became one of the youngest crew members in his squadron, where he worked as a radio and electronic countermeasures operator. After attending City College in San Francisco, he joined the S.F.P.D., serving as a police officer and undercover agent for four years before joining the well-known Hal Lipset Investigative firm as vice-president. From there, he went on to start Buckman and Associates. His new firm immediately attracted wealthy and famous clientele; like Dean Martin, Frank Sinatra's attorney Melvin Belli, and Israeli Prime Minister Golda Meir. The firm handled cases involving litigation over trade secret theft, recovering hidden assets and helping a client escape war-torn Yugoslavia. Buckman & Associates had achieved results for clients in over 20 countries.

Buckman was probably best known for his work in international child recovery: he'd been credited with the successful recovery of over 100 children from around the world. He was also known to be one of the highest compensated private investigators in the nation, as I would soon find out firsthand. He was selective about the cases he took, and I believe my source had a lot to do with his consideration of my case. If you didn't have child custody orders, Buckman wouldn't talk to you. His team did not carry weapons when recovering children. Very rarely was he in his office, but he could be reached almost immediately anywhere in the world by his staff. He had given interviews on numerous television talk shows. It was said that he had sold the rights to his life story to a film production company for an undisclosed amount.

Understandably, I was impressed by the man's dossier, but I began to worry that he was out of my league. He initially kicked around a figure of $30,000 but couldn't be sure until he went to Xalapa to check things out for himself. I figured the initial figure was loose change for a guy like this. I worried about what his final figure would be.

Buckman was down in Xalapa for a week. On a Wednesday night he called me from Xalapa. "Your source was accurate. I'll be back in town on Monday," was the only thing he would say over the phone.

We got together almost immediately after his return. The trip went well. My parents sat in as we all listened intensely to what he'd found.

"I was watching the home early in the morning when a VW van full of kids pulled up, and Stephen walked out from the steel door near the garage and climbed into the side door of the van."

"You actually saw Stephen?" I asked, sitting up in my chair, my heart pounding.

"How did he look? Are you sure it was him?" I asked.

He laid out two photos on the large dining table. "Here's the house, and here's the bus," he replied. "Only one boy left the house, and I recognized him from the pictures you gave me. He seems fine. I followed the bus to the next pickup and then on to the school where the van dropped the kids off. Everything you told me about the airfield checked out.

"It operates from dawn to dusk, but I couldn't get access to the field because of filming for a movie called *Clear and Present Danger*. Security was tight because the U.S. Air Force had provided some Blackhawk Helicopters for the shooting, so the field was closed to the public. I talked to some of the film crew, getting rowdy at a local bar. They told me the field wouldn't be open again for about three or four weeks."

Having not even discussed the costs I felt this new delay was a big setback. We would now have to wait more than a month to launch the rescue. The only other option was an overland escape and that scenario was one I hoped not to undertake.

Buckman had timed distances and studied traffic flow over several routes through Xalapa. By the time he left, he knew the town better than I did, and he had also selected a particular escape route.

"The rescue is more complex than I had originally figured. We will need extra help, including a Mexican federal policeman who will do it for a fee. I've talked with a pilot who has his own plane and is willing to go. It all means that it is going to cost much more than the $30,000 figure that I estimated initially," Buckman explained.

"How much more are we talking about?" I reluctantly asked with a lump in my throat.

"$21,000 more," he replied.

The rescue drifted and popped in front of me like a delicate soap bubble. I could feel Stephen slipping away from me. I looked at my dad, but the figure had not defeated him. Dad was direct and firm with his words.

"Does the entire amount need to be given up front?" he asked.

"Tom," Buckman said. "I know it's a lot of money, but we need specialized help to get us all out of there while the authorities are still trying to figure out what happened. The pilot and plane alone will eat up a substantial chunk. If we tried to drive out, an overland route by car is still 14 hours from the closest U.S. point of entry in Brownsville. If the Mexicans are sophisticated enough and the grandfather is as well connected as I believe he is, a drive-out would be very high risk."

"Let's do it then," Dad said.

"Dad, you know I don't have that kind of money, and I can't let my problem eat up your retirement," I argued.

My mother, Hilda, the quiet anchor in our large family, is tiny and gentle, but you don't want to cross her where the family is concerned. She had been sitting quietly at my father's side, but now she looked at me and said, "We'll manage. We need to get Stevie home." My father turned to me to explain their position.

"A lot of people are interested in seeing Stevie home. I consider this a family matter, and when families come together, good things happen. It's time to bring Stevie home," he said.

I was beyond gratitude for the immense moral support I had received from my parents, but I certainly hadn't intended to expose them to the devastating costs. In theory the rescue seemed possible, but I knew that "attempt" was the operative word with zero guarantees. There would never be a second chance. If things went wrong, not only would I probably never see my Son again, but

BROKEN TREATY

I'd be paying back the money for years, regardless of the outcome. The agreement also stipulated that I would have to pay legal fees for Buckman and Associates if any litigation arose--a matter I considered to be the least of my worries at this time. I never wavered on what was the right thing to do; I just considered the downside.

We established a payment arrangement with Buckman. The final payment was to be rendered one week before I was to meet up with Pat in Xalapa.

BROKEN TREATY

Chapter 12

Adopting a Disguise

I had concerns about the weather In Xalapa, which would be changing soon. In late April and on into the summer, huge thunderheads build in the gulf that could ground our plane. We needed to fly at 10,000 feet, an altitude that would allow us to stay over international waters yet enable us to glide to a landing on a beach if our engine failed. We would also be running with the plane's transponder switched off to avoid detection. We needed good visibility for VFR (Visual Flight Rules), and to watch for any other aircraft that might be interested in us.

At the beginning of March, only two weeks before the planned rescue, I was helping a lady friend recover her luggage at a baggage claim at SFO airport. She tugged on my sleeve to point out Marc Klass, the father of young Polly Klass who had been taken from her home in the middle of the night in Petaluma, California, and murdered on a quiet dirt road outside the town. The story had been headline news since the murder in October of 1993; 10 months after Stephen had been taken to Mexico.

"You should talk to him about your situation. I'll bet he could guide you to someone who could help," Adrienne suggested. Adrienne was only too familiar with Stephens' disappearance. But I hadn't told her about the rescue we were planning. The rescue plan had been kept within the family.

"I don't think he wants to be bothered, especially after all he's been through," I said. I dismissed the notion of approaching him about Stephen.

"Steve, you should go and talk to him now while he's just waiting," she urged again. I gathered some courage and carefully made my way toward the man who carried the broken heart of a nation. He shouldered an unimaginable level of personal suffering. I moved toward him, but stopped only a few feet away. His face was expressionless and seemed incapable of anything but the numb, frozen exterior of grief. At that moment I realized that he didn't need to be bothered with another man's problem. For the first time since being forced into the role of a left-behind parent, I now saw the eyes of an "ultimate loss" with wounds that would never heal.

I realized how fortunate I was knowing that my son was alive and that I still had a small chance to see him home. The encounter put everything into perspective and I let Mr. Klass be. He and his daughter would be in my thoughts during my attempt to bring Stephen home.

As the target date drew nearer, my meetings with Buckman became more frequent. On our last meeting, just before the plan was to be set in motion, I voiced my concern that my son might be out of school for Easter break on the intended day of the rescue. Buckman was confident, certain it wouldn't be an issue. The intuition was so strong that I insisted it be double checked by having someone call the school in Xalapa to verify. There was too much at stake.

The next night Buckman called me. My hunch paid off. The school would be shut down for two weeks during the break. Classes wouldn't resume until April 11. From that point on, Buckman listened more carefully to my input.

April 11 became our revised rescue target date, but Buckman and the pilot, understanding my concerns about the changing weather pattern in Veracruz, realized that the window for favorable weather to fly in or out of Xalapa was closing. I knew from living down there that late spring brought afternoon showers nearly as reliable as a Swiss clock.

In previous meetings, I mentioned reservations about being recognized by Silvia's family or anyone else who might know me. I remembered how quickly we had been discovered when I visited Xalapa with my dad and sisters in June.

"Why don't you just grow a full beard," he suggested. "It will probably help you get over your paranoia about being recognized."

I had about a month to grow the beard. Once it filled out, I trimmed and died it a dark brown. I also tanned my skin as dark as I could get it in the tanning booth and had some glasses made up with only enough tinting in the lenses to hide my eye color but not look like sunglasses.

Predictably, my Hague petition was still going nowhere, and I learned that the MCA was severely under-funded and operated on a barely sustainable budget. It occurred to me that maybe the staff was comprised of interns, which would explain why the faces in the office seemed so young.

The ineffectiveness of the MCA was developing into an unexpected advantage for me: The fourth pickup had been thwarted and sent back to Mexico City. Silvia was probably letting her guard down, figuring I was eagerly awaiting the results of the next pickup order. But I wasn't waiting anymore.

Using the "amparo" legal loophole, Silvia had secured a federal Mexican court injunction at the state court level in Veracruz, frustrating the Hague process. Peña and his office again prepared legal orders overriding that decision and expected the next attempt now in early April, only a week and a half before the planned rescue attempt. I silently held out a last desperate hope that somehow the MCA attempt would succeed and that Melanie would be given instructions to head to Mexico City. If this happened, I might still have time to nullify my agreement with Buckman. In reality, I knew that the remote possibility Peña's office could pull this off now was just a dream and I blamed myself for letting it go on for 15 months.

At times I felt like curling up into a ball and confronting my anger and loneliness. But I wouldn't allow myself the luxury of a good cry until I had given up complete hope of ever seeing Stephen again. Hope meant I still had a chance. I hadn't been defeated, and as details were refined and the rescue drew nearer, I grew quieter, not mentioning the rescue to a soul, but I felt like I was beginning to climb out of my own tomb.

A few weeks before the final projected rescue date, I left the jobsite early on a Sunday afternoon to shop for some clothing for Stephen. He would need to change out of his school uniform to avoid drawing interest from any authorities during the rescue, especially on the airfield. I went to the Macy's boys department and bought a sweatshirt some shirts and a pair of jeans. I passed over the tennis shoes. Sadly, I could only guess at his sizes, not sure how much he had grown during the last 16 months.

While at the mall, I wandered into a gift shop that caught my interest. I was drawn to a shelf covered with small hand-carved wooden planes. I found two identical, fist-size planes and bought them both. I had been putting together an Easter package to send to

BROKEN TREATY

Stephen, even though I doubted he'd ever see it. I carefully wrapped one of the planes in simple newspaper and placed it in the box going to Xalapa. It was a symbolic act.

BROKEN TREATY

Chapter 13

Let's bring Stephen home

A red-eye flight put me into Mexico City at 5:30 a.m. I pushed the tinted glasses over my eyes before leaving the plane. In the past, I have run into people who knew me from Xalapa in the same airport. I could never fool anyone, but I tried to look less like an American.

Three hours later, wheels were down at the Veracruz airport. I had kept fluent with my Spanish, using it daily at my work with employees. Your dialect or accent reveals your origin or where you learned to speak Spanish. I learned in Puebla but adopted somewhat of a Xalapan accent from my wife and her family and friends.

At the airport, I entered a rental car agency and chose a Volkswagen sedan. Four doors was a must by Buckman's request. If things went according to plan, I would never see this rental agency again, and they would have to send someone back up to Xalapa to retrieve the car when we were done with it.

The heat and humidity in Veracruz were tremendous. I set out on the drive to Xalapa along the two-lane, winding highway. I figured it would be cooler in Xalapa, which was above 4,000 feet, but I was wrong. The longer I drove up this highway, the stronger the sun beat down at a more direct angle. It was a good hour and a half drive from Veracruz to Xalapa.

I recognized some of the usual mini-markets, restaurants and refreshment stands we had so often frequented during the many drives with Silvia's family in years long gone.

BROKEN TREATY

I had a terrible tension headache welling up from the anxiety and hoped I might find a motel soon enough to sneak in a nap before a prearranged meeting at Pat's hotel at 6:00 p.m.

I ruled out a hotel in town to minimize the possibility of being recognized. I had something else in mind. Every town in Mexico has motels on the outskirts that Mexican wives deplore. "No-tell motels" are designed to accommodate mostly married men and their girlfriends or prostitutes. On the highway a few miles south of Xalapa, I spotted the "Auto Motel" and turned in. Each room has its own garage with a large curtain to cover the garage opening to offer optimum discretion. I would have found humor in the manager's reaction if my purpose had been less crucial—needing a room for a few days instead of a few hours. He didn't seem to have a problem, though, but glanced curiously at my car to see why I had not brought a woman along. The motel accepted cash only, and the fee was $20 dollars a day. There was no registration card to fill out, which suited me just fine.

The heat was brutal. Scorching vapor radiated from walls and pavement. With no air-conditioning, a nap during the afternoon was not possible. Buckman was adamant about a "no phone" policy, cell or otherwise. With no way to communicate over the last few days, I wondered if any plans had changed or if any of team members had not made the trip.

I needed to stop thinking about the circumstances that put me in the loneliest place and time I'd known in my 35 years. It was time to relinquish control and have faith in the best option I had. I would be where and when I was expected, holding on to the only "real" chance to bring Stephen home.

Chapter 14

The master plan

Buckman approached as I got out of my Volkswagen. He wore khaki slacks with a white casual dress shirt that added a rich contrast to his tanned face. He is a seasoned sailor, and I learned that in one rescue he had sailed a mother and her rescued daughter out of Puerto Vallarta back to California on his own boat. It gave me confidence to know that his rescue methods were as different as the cases he took.

"You're a little late, but that's okay," he said. My watch showed seven minutes after the hour. The hotel didn't exist the last time I was in Xalapa; I had to double back twice to find it. Seeing him meticulous about time gave me more confidence.

"You look like a drug smuggler with that beard," he said, motioning me in a direction toward the back of the hotel. He seemed to want to move out of view of the highway just beyond the parking lot. Buckman went to great lengths to avoid being seen with me. I could have learned much about details in advance if we could have traveled together. I assumed that much of what had been engineered would be on a need-to-know-basis. Phone contact was out of the question and didn't matter since I had no phone in my room; the only amenity being complimentary porn, piped-in from the front desk. It held no interest for me.

I wouldn't meet the pilot until tomorrow when a local pleasure flight had been scheduled as a dry run for the rescue. I did know the pilot's name, Ed, since we had to cut a separate check for $13,000 for his part in the rescue. Aside from another associate named Mike, I did not know who else was involved. Buckman had asked me to submit a request written to Mike's parole officer explaining that we needed his help to clear up a matter in another state and that he would be gone for about a week. He also told me not to worry, since Mike's issue was white-collar related only.

The purpose of the "pleasure" flight the next morning would be twofold: One, to get the authorities and guards at the airport accustomed to our coming and going, and two, to familiarize procedures and systems on the aircraft. Aircraft and aviation, however, were not foreign to me. Some years back, before going away to college in Mexico, I learned to fly Cessnas; logging roughly fifty hours of flight time, training in Cessna 150s. I could fly, but the low-wing Cherokee was foreign to me.

Buckman and I made our way to the back of the hotel where it was quiet. He was all business. He spoke and I listened carefully as we continued walking at a slower pace.

"There's a change from the original plan. We'll fly directly to Brownsville, Texas, instead of Guatemala," he said.

I felt as if some of the pressure inside my head had been released as the potential for a three-way international custody skirmish in Guatemala was suddenly removed.

"Ed refueled the Cherokee after landing in Veracruz. I met him at the airport where we filled two five-gallon cans of aviation fuel and brought them in the trunk of my rental car. The Cherokee is tied up down the road at El Lencero," he said.

The place is completely quiet, only soldiers standing in the shade and some officials in and around the tower.

BROKEN TREATY

The fact that El Lencero had no fuel was our dilemma, considering the fuel range of the Cherokee. Ten gallons of gas in a car trunk would allow us to make it to Brownsville with enough reserve fuel instead of a 180 degree heading toward Guatemala, about half the distance.

"The federal cop we hired is being baby sat in a hotel room with one of our people until we need him Monday morning," he explained. "He will detain the school van while you get Stephen out of the van and into your car driven by another driver. The federale will then present a copy of the pickup order that you gave us from the Mexican Central Authority. He'll also present a translated copy of the custody order from California. The paperwork has all kinds of official stamps and seals all over it, so it should be completely convincing." Buckman paused to see if I still followed.

"The cop will then instruct the driver to go on ahead to the school, Las Hayas, with the other children in the van and give the documents to the school staff, giving us time to get to the airfield where Ed will have the Cherokee pre-flighted and be waiting on the tarmac," Buckman explained.

"How much time will we have if the police get involved?" I asked.

"If the van goes on to the school, we'll probably be in the air before the cops arrive at the school and take a police report. If the van doesn't move and someone calls the police, we still will have some time because a policeman will have to take a report before any high level search is initiated. Police always arrive to investigate before any decisive action is initiated--it's the same in every city in every country. We will probably have at least half an hour to get to the plane, a good 20 minutes away depending on Monday morning traffic, which I've already factored in," he said.

I shouldn't have expected any less meticulous preparation, but this was the first time that I saw anyone performing beyond a mouthful of rhetoric in a previously hopeless situation. I didn't have any questions, but began to understand that the plan was more intricate than I had imagined. We split up with arrangements to meet in the morning.

The next morning, I arrived early to try to eat something in the restaurant at Buckman's hotel. I sat a few tables away from where he ate breakfast with another man who I assumed was Ed, our pilot. I had been instructed not to speak to or acknowledge them.

The two men left their table and walked out of the restaurant. I waited five minutes before settling my bill and walked a block up the highway to sit on the curb as if waiting for a bus. On Sundays, the only day of rest for most Mexicans, mornings are ghostly quiet. I was outrageously out of place, but drew little interest. From my left, a large sedan pulled off the street and slowed to a stop in the loose rocks and dirt a few feet from me. A rear door of the green Lincoln Town Car swung open and I climbed into the back seat.

Buckman introduced me to the pilot by first name only. Ed was about my stature; 5' 9" and 160 lbs. He had brown hair and a goatee and looked to be in his early forties.

"I can't tell you how much I appreciate your help down here, Ed."

His help hadn't come cheap, but there was significant risk. I speculated that he believed Buckman's engineering was either bulletproof, or that his understanding of the consequences were less than realistic. I had nothing to lose, but Ed risked his freedom and

BROKEN TREATY

his Cherokee if things went bad.

"You get your boy to my plane and I'll fly us out of here," Ed said, with a hint of cockiness.

The Lincoln headed southeast away from Xalapa toward the airfield. Within 10 minutes, we were at the security gate leading to the field. A guard recognized the vehicle, offering a broad smile as he lifted the thin black and white striped barrier arm. I noticed an old .38 revolver at his side. Since landing Buckman and Ed had been making friends at the field by giving away bags of beef jerky to some of the guards.

Buckman and I walked to the plane while Ed went to explain to the field master that we were just going for a short sightseeing flight. As we began unbuttoning the canopy cover, two soldiers approached us carrying rifles.

"Did you forget to give someone their beef jerky, Pat?" I asked.

He saw no humor in my comment. He instead turned his back to the soldiers as if to shield his instructions to me.

"Don't let them know that you speak Spanish. Just listen to what they say to each other. I want to know if they are suspicious about anything, so listen carefully," he said – his face just inches from mine.

A short, heavy-set soldier handed Buckman a torn piece of paper with some figures scratched on it. Buckman realized they had added a zero to the daily fee, trying to charge ten times the usual amount. With Ed now back from the field master's office, the two soldiers, Buckman and Ed got into an almost amusing squabble over a few dollars. Ed finally settled the matter with a 10-dollar bill, and the two soldiers went away happy. Among the soldiers' comments to

BROKEN TREATY

each other, I heard nothing said to indicate that they were suspicious of us.

As we taxied to the far end of the runway, Buckman handed me a headset and instructed me to listen for anything unusual being said in the tower. Once in the air, he explained where Stephen and I would seat our selves, and how our bags should be stowed. Because of weight and balance considerations, it was decided that I would sit behind Ed, and Stephen would be on my right, just behind Buckman. I was shown the makeshift urinal, an empty gallon milk jug.

"We'll probably more likely need something to shit in when this goes down," Ed commented. Rather than finding humor in his wisecrack, it reminded me of the bizarre turns my life had taken.

Flying in a long counterclockwise sweep about 1,500 feet above the terrain, we encountered only moderate turbulence from hot air updrafts as the cloudless morning sky ripened for another searing day. Cloudless days like this, at any time of year, were unusual in Xalapa, "almost out of balance," I thought.

Below us was a tangled carpet of jungle. Most of the landscape was mountain or valley with any carved-out flat areas devoted to coffee, jalapeño peppers, vanilla and mango. As Ed guided the craft back toward the field, aligning the plane for final approach, I allowed myself to consider that maybe 24 hours from now, I could be flying out of here with Stephen sitting next to me. The notion made my eyes water. We returned to the field and topped off the tanks with the two gas cans from the trunk of the Lincoln.

After securing the Cherokee, and on our way toward the gate, Ed asked to stop when we saw a twin-engine Piper Aztec plane that sat alone conspicuously in front of the field master's office. The tires were flat, and the Plexiglass on the cockpit was so thick with dust that no view into the cockpit was possible. Heavy-gage chain with padlocks crisscrossed the wings and wrapped around each of the propeller blades -- a slow death for the once magnificent Aztec.

Ed was determined to learn about the plane's history and neglected condition, and went inside to talk to the field master. He returned several minutes later looking nervous. He learned that the plane had been confiscated and the pilot imprisoned for criminal behavior. Ed said little after that, even abandoning his cynicism.

Up the highway, just before re-entering the city, we came upon dozens of police cars lit up like Christmas trees parked along the shoulders of the roadway. I read the large banner on one of the buses.

"It's a presidential candidate on a campaign. I think they've stepped-up protection since the assassination last month of the presidential candidate in Tijuana," I told them.

They would be gone tomorrow, we told ourselves, but Ed remained quiet and heavy in thought. I didn't want to think about what I would do it if Ed started making noise about flying out before the rescue.

Buckman dropped me back at my car near his hotel well before noon. Before driving away, he instructed me on what time to meet later that evening for a dry run over the rescue route. We also wanted to review crucial details of tomorrow morning's plan. I returned to my motel room with nothing left to do but lay on the bed, sweating, hoping for some kind of relief. The heat was so rare in this city that ceiling fans hadn't been a consideration – let alone air conditioning.

BROKEN TREATY

We met at 7 p.m. The city was relatively quiet. I was shown the route to the spot where I would drive my Volkswagen early the next morning to wait for the other team member I still hadn't met. I assumed it was the same man babysitting the cop.

"You will follow me to this rendezvous point. Mike will get out of his car and immediately get behind the wheel of your Volkswagen while you move to the passenger seat. Mike will then drive to a location one and a half blocks from Alberto's house and wait for me to give you the signal that Stephen is on the van. After following the van to its next stop, your car will park behind the van and I will park in front of the van," he explained.

I listened intently, fully focused, watching his mouth, to make sure the voice matched his lip movement hoping not to miss a thing as the details were recited.

"The cop riding with me will then approach the door of the van, with you following him. When the cop hands over the documents, you will lift your son out of the van and explain to Stephen that the policeman is there to help us get him home. You will then get back into the Volkswagen with your son. Mike will drive you to the first car-switch location where we will leave your car and drive away in the second vehicle. Is that clear?" Buckman asked.

"Yes," I replied, trying to put a visual in my head of my precise role in the rescue.

Buckman was taking me over the exact route planned for the morning. He now steered the Lincoln in the direction of Alberto's home, where Stephen would board the van and drive to the next stop where we would make the rescue. The closer we got the more anxious and vulnerable I felt. I was tempted to duck for fear of being noticed. While driving, Buckman continued to explain in detail what driver would be where in reference to the school van's position when it was to pick up Stephen. I heard his words, but I couldn't fully process their meaning. As we turned another corner closer to the home, my heart pounded, and I found myself scrambling for my baseball cap. Keeping up with his explicit instructions challenged my comprehension. After each important detail, I tried to repeat what he was telling me so he could correct me if I misunderstood. One consolation was that I wouldn't be driving after Mike took the wheel of my car. I knew the car-switch and ride to the airfield would be very emotional for me and confusing for Stephen.

Buckman made a turn I wasn't prepared for. Now we were driving directly past Alberto's home. We drove at a less hurried pace than other vehicles on the street. As we passed in front of the house, my fear shrank when I realized I was probably within fifty yards of Stephen. He was just behind the steel-door entrance and concrete walls that encircled the home. I wasn't quite sure how I would react if I saw him playing outside or walking with treats from one of the neighborhood tiendas.

The entrance to the home was closed, and the street empty. No cars were parked outside. The entire city had a serene quiet exaggerated by the Indian summer-like condition I knew back home in California. The evening was hot, but now tolerable, with a lingering sun setting slowly behind the backdrop of enormous mountain peaks. Kids were going to bed a little earlier that night since their vacation was coming to a close. Dusk was settling in on this Sunday night. No sign of Stephen – though in a strange way I felt his presence and knew he was behind those walls.

BROKEN TREATY

As we drove by the home, I wondered if by chance he hadn't paused to think of me and wonder whatever happened to the father who made the ultimate promise to bring him home. We rounded a corner and my daydream closed. We turned down the boulevard that would lead to the school van's next stop after picking Stephen up from Alberto's house in less than 12 hours.

My mind had drifted though Buckman hadn't stopped going over details. I began to repeat details and instructions, trusting he would correct me if I got something wrong.

We proceeded on to where the actual pickup would take place; a horseshoe shaped street directly off the main avenue. Buckman's review was so intricate that I struggled to follow. He had spent countless hours studying, tracking and timing. At almost every stoplight, he glanced at his watch to time the light for both red and green. We turned onto the street where we would recover Stephen. His choreographed moves were dependent on the dancers learning the steps.

"What happens with the cop," I asked.

"He's on his own after the recovery. He knows nothing about Ed and the plane and only knows me and Mike by our first names."

We headed back to his hotel. He reconfirmed the meeting time for 6:30 a.m. the next morning, at the same place we'd met him this morning, only tomorrow I would be driving my VW, following him into town. We wouldn't be talking again before then.

Instead of going directly back to my motel, I decided to head on down the highway to look for something to eat. As I passed my motel I noticed that business was brisk even though it was Sunday night. All the curtains were drawn across the carports. Twenty kilometers down the highway, I found a roadside restaurant and tried to force some food down.

By 10 p.m. I was back in my room. I spent an hour or so organizing my gear so I would have Stephen's change of clothes and documents easily within reach. I arranged and rearranged everything several times. I spend a ridiculous amount of time on this but it calmed it down. I was nervous and scared about what tomorrow would bring. I wasn't worried for myself. If I couldn't get Stephen headed back home with me tomorrow, I really didn't care much about the future. I only knew that there could never be any hope of a diplomatic resolution if we got caught. Before going to sleep I set two alarms as a precaution.

At midnight I slept.

BROKEN TREATY

BROKEN TREATY

Chapter 15

Losing our Federale

I was awake long before the first alarm sounded at 5:15 a.m. By 6:00 a.m. it was still dark, but the heat was tolerable. My garage entrance was the only one with a curtain still drawn across it indicating I was the last guest. I had my gear in the car. I awakened the night attendant sleeping on the floor in the manager's office and asked him to hold my key for me until I returned later, a precaution in the event things didn't go as planned this morning. I didn't want them to rent my room when the maid saw my bags gone.

I arrived a few minutes early at the rendezvous point. Buckman was already waiting. Before I could shut off the engine, he appeared at my window. The look in his eyes indicated a problem.

"Our federale was called back to Mexico City last night – he's gone. You're the only one of us that speaks fluent Spanish. We have to call it off unless you'd be willing to take his place. Will you do it?" he asked.

Buckman knew I would do it, but presented it in a way that would let me opt out if I wasn't up to it or now had a change of heart.

"Yes, of course," I replied without hesitation. The direction of my involvement, from passive to active had become strangely appropriate. I was grateful that I had only been made aware of the cop's disappearance at that moment, rather than worrying about my new role through the night.

Buckman explained that the other team member who would drive my car had some kind of official looking badge to flash at the driver as we approached the van, but would stand back while I introduced documents and gave instructions to the driver. I wasn't comfortable trying to impersonate a policeman, since it might make things worse for the others if we got caught.

On the drive to the second rendezvous location where Mike waited, I would have about 10 minutes to consider the problem. I handed my bags to Buckman to toss through the rear door of his car. I followed him through town to the street where I was to wait. He went on to inform the others that the rescue would go as planned.

Buckman's day had begun earlier than mine. At 5:30, he and Ed had gone to the field to unbutton the plane and file a phony flight plan to Poza Rica, a completely different compass heading than the direction of Brownsville, our actual destination. The tower personnel had insisted on knowing the names of the passengers; a sign they were taking interest in our movements. Buckman had left Ed at the field to do his preflight check. The officials were told that we were leaving today. Ed would fiddle about on the aircraft until we arrived. Having no car at the field meant no way out, and if we got caught, he wouldn't know it until he was suddenly grounded by the tower.

I arrived at the meeting location first, and considered my options regarding the policeman impersonation while I waited for the others. I decided it was best not to mention the word "police." If I could muster fast bursts in my best Spanish, and heavily armed with arrogance, I might at least create enough confusion while handing over documents. I would have Mike with his security badge distract the driver while I lifted Stephen out of the van.

BROKEN TREATY

Behind the green Town Car, a white Topaz followed. I figured this was the other team member. He parked and emerged to cross the street toward my car. He was surprisingly youthful looking, about 32-years-old, a little younger than I. He was shorter than average, had a slender build, and came across rather innocent-looking. I figured that this was Mike, the man whose parole officer I had written a letter to asking to have his absence excused.

I scrambled out of the driver's seat, and as we passed each other around the front of the car, he greeted me by name and introduced himself as "Mike." Once we were seated, he started the engine to follow Buckman's sedan back into traffic toward Alberto's house where we expected Stephen to get on the school van. During the brief ride, I explained how I intended to handle the driver. I realized that Mike's part in the rescue was supposed to be nothing more than a driver. I asked if he had a pair of sunglasses to look more like a cop. He did not. I remembered the pair I had in my bag in Buckman's car, but there would be no time to retrieve them now.

My heart raced as we neared the spot where Stephen should be getting on the small bus. Mike and I parked a block and a half up from Albertos' house as planned. A red Thunderbird sped up the street from behind us, then turned onto the boulevard. I only caught a brief glimpse from the side, but I was sure it was Silvia with her father behind the wheel.

"Did you see that red Thunderbird drive by?" I asked Mike.

"Yeah, why?" he said, not taking his eyes off the street in both directions, watching for the yellow and black school van that would stop at the house.

"I think that was my wife with her Dad driving in that car," I

BROKEN TREATY

replied.

"Does her father wear glasses?" Mike asked.

"Only when he drives, and he is also mostly bald," I added.

"Well, that was probably them," he said.

Buckman was now in position on the opposite side of the street about fifty yards closer to the home, with a good vantage point to watch as Stephen boarded the van. He would then signal, driving past us giving a "yes" or "no" head movement.

Mike and I saw the black and yellow Volkswagen van approach as anticipated, but we had an obscured view. Aware of my own anxiety, I took deep measured breaths trying to pace my heart rate. The van stopped in front of the house and gave two long blasts from the horn. I was perhaps moments away from holding and speaking with my son. We now waited for Buckman to confirm that Stephen got on the van. Two minutes passed while the van idled in front of the house. Finally an employee from the tortilleria next to the house approached the van and said something to the driver. The van made a U-turn and drove past us. I looked to see if any of the children's faces might be Stephen's. I didn't see my son. We waited for Buckman to drive up and explain what had just happened. Pulling his car over in front of us, he came up to my window, looking distraught.

"He never got on the van," he said. "I had a completely unobstructed view of the entry, and he did not come out."

"Pat, I'm pretty sure we saw Silvia and her father driving past us in a red Thunderbird," I said.

"That's strange because no vehicles left the house," Buckman said.

The look on Buckman's face suggested that this scenario was

completely unexpected and he didn't like being out of control. Time was wasting and we needed to make decisions fast.

"Let's follow the bus to the school and see if he gets off the van there. Maybe he was to be picked up at another stop," I reasoned.

"I don't have a better idea right now," Buckman said.

I was concerned that Stephen was in the Thunderbird with his mom being driven to school by Alberto. Perhaps I'd somehow been spotted. I also had wondered if Silvia simply hadn't gotten Stephen up in time to make it to school.

Mike and I hurried down the avenue behind Buckman's Lincoln, toward the winding road that led to the school. As we passed the bus, I looked again for Stephen but couldn't see his face. A few kilometers farther along, Buckman pulled over and came to my window.

"This is pointless," he said flatly. "Neither your son nor any vehicle left the house during any time I watched." The tone in Buckman's voice was as if this was just a minor setback and that the plan only needed some fine tuning.

I was losing confidence, feeling as though we'd lost our one shot, my anxiety was turning to depression, causing me to feel numb and become silent.

"We all need to break up now before we start looking suspicious. Steve, you and I will meet later around 12:30 to go over what happened and the options we still have. I've got to get back to the airfield where Ed is waiting and explain to the field master why we're not flying today. They seem awfully eager for us to get out of here. We're going to have to tell them something creative," Buckman said.

BROKEN TREATY

It was now nearing 8:30 a.m. I was dropped off at my car and headed back to my motel.

I was glad I'd told the management I'd be back. I sat on the bed, pondering the morning's events. I wondered if I'd been spotted in town, alerting Silvia. If this were the case, they would no longer be at Alberto's house and Stephen would be kept from school.

I met Buckman at 12:30. This time I swung by for him in front of his hotel and we drove down the highway away from town and discuss our options. I could tell he was troubled about our setback today and had already begun engineering a new approach.

We drove to the roadside restaurant I'd found the night before. The heat was starting up again. I watched a ceiling fan spin around at the table next to us as a squadron of flies seemed to enjoy riding the spiraling downdraft created by the blades.

We talked about what might have gone wrong. What if Silvia had taken Stephen out of school or moved to another home?

"Something isn't right. He should have been on the van. It was the first day back to school after a two-week vacation. Your Son should have been on the van," he said again. After a pause, I shared my thoughts.

"I think Silvia may have overslept and not gotten him up for school."

"What kind of mother would oversleep and let her kid miss school?" He eyed me in disbelief.

"I know her well, believe me. It's possible, and probably what happened." I paused for a moment and then continued.

"Look, Pat, I know this family. They love to stay up as late as three or four in the morning playing cards and talking and then sleep into the afternoon, kind of like living at Graceland. They used to do this on all of the vacations I spent with them. The sobering reality of getting out of bed early for work or school didn't dawn on them until they crossed that fine line between Sunday night and Monday morning," I reasoned.

Buckman listened, but I could see he didn't accept it.

"We'll know more tomorrow. As careful as we've been, no one that matters knows we're in town and what we're doing here," he said.

I didn't have the heart to tell him I had exchanged some dollars for pesos at his hotel and foolishly signed my name on a receipt. It could link us together down the road.

Our conversation turned toward Ed and the plane.

"When I got back to the field, the officials were getting a little suspicious that we weren't going through with our flight plan. Luckily, the field master can speak a little English, and I told to him that you had gotten food poisoning and were down for the count, and that we would fly tomorrow instead. They asked a lot of questions and recommended leaving you and going on.

"I bet it didn't make Ed any less paranoid," I tossed in.

"No, it didn't. He's convinced we're all going to get caught and he's going to lose his plane. I explained to the field master that you've never been to Poza Rica and would be devastated if left behind. Ed and I realized that we can't get away with another no-fly tomorrow. The field master will probably ground the plane and call the police if we don't fly tomorrow. The plane will have to leave in the morning whether or not we are aboard," he revealed.

BROKEN TREATY

My morale was hitting new lows as each disappointing twist in the rescue unraveled. First, we lost the cop. Then, Stephen didn't get on the van. And now we would lose the plane in the morning. Everything depended on Stephen getting on that van tomorrow.

Buckman and I explored other options. Looking at a map together, we considered a drive-out rescue along the coast. The drive would take 14 hours. I admired Buckman's willingness to remain devoted to getting Stephen out. He could have been safely on the next commercial flight out of Veracruz the moment things went sour, but he would let the plane go and stick around for a surface scramble to the border with Stephen and me if it came to that.

Buckman didn't take foolish risks though. He confided that he had given a retainer of $2,000 to a high-profile attorney in Mexico City to bail him out should the need occur. I didn't ask if that included me since I didn't care much what happened to me if things went south. If it meant never seeing my son again, I figured I'd be better off being taken out to a remote spot and quietly taken care of. The grief was taking too much of a toll on me physically and psychologically.

As I tried to force down the last of my eggs, Buckman suddenly asked, "Would you be willing to remove your son from the classroom? And do you think you could get to the car with him?"

"Yes, I could." I would have little control, however, after that if authorities became interested enough to set up roadblocks on the highway toward Brownsville, I thought to myself.

We left the restaurant and headed back toward Xalapa. We decided to meet again at 6:30 p.m. for another dry run and to take a look at a back road that would bring us to the highway, completely circumventing the city. This would be an option if we resorted to picking Stephen up at school.

When I dropped Buckman off, I asked him if he thought it would be okay to make a call home from the hotel desk in the lobby. He said yes but insisted that I had to be careful what I said because the international operators sometimes listen in on calls to see if the line had cleared, and most international operators spoke English. I gave him time to get to his room before I entered the hotel.

At the reception desk, I made a collect call using a nickname that my dad would recognize. He accepted the charges.

"Dad, the fishing wasn't good today, but my fishing guide says we'll try again tomorrow, hopefully with better luck. The plane that we planned to return from fishing on, has to leave tomorrow, but we may try to keep fishing a little longer and even drive home if we are lucky," I explained.

There was a brief pause on the other end, then a slow and clear response. "I understand," my father replied.

"If you don't hear from me tomorrow, just assume I'm staying here awhile until the fishing gets better," I added. He acknowledged what I said, but suddenly I broke away from my cipher. "Dad, I'm really scared that we won't get Stephen out."

I didn't need to explain. He knew there probably wasn't going to be a second shot at bringing Stephen home.

"I know," he answered, his voice compassionate, yet solemn.

I drew strength from his calmness. My dad was very close to Stephen, and both he and my mom were torn apart over Stephen's disappearance. Not knowing how I would survive my own failure, I didn't know how to handle their inevitable devastation.

BROKEN TREATY

I said goodbye to my Dad. He insisted that I not lose hope and wished me luck.

I returned to the solitude of the vacant motel. No guests, just the cleaning ladies. Knowing what they must know about the place, I was surprised that latex gloves weren't standard issue. By now, the staff had probably stopped trying to figure me out and seemed to accept me as a misguided tourist. I was cordial to them, and they were friendly to me in return. It was time for siesta. I did my best to sleep during the hottest hours of the afternoon.

Buckman and I met up later, as planned. Once again, we headed toward Alberto's house and drove the route to the planned recovery spot. He pointed out where Mike and I would be parked and waiting on the horseshoe shaped street, the last stop for the school van before it arrived at the school. There wasn't much difference from the original plan, only that Mike and I wouldn't wait near Alberto's house as we had done this morning. Buckman was continually noting times and kilometers between points and adjusting them for morning rush hour traffic. He took particular notice of police stations, transit cops, and timed traffic lights.

We headed back to the highway, then toward the airfield turning where we believed the road would take us toward the school from the back road. Buckman called out minutes and counted out kilometers as we drove. We finally intersected with the road from the school. The route did, however, add 10 minutes to the drive to the airfield if we decided to try a schoolyard rescue. But we could at least avoid having to drive through town where the authorities might be alerted.

We would only attempt a schoolyard rescue if Stephen didn't get on the van. In that case, we would figure he was living at another home and hope he was still attending the same school. We would then make an attempt only if I could locate him somewhere in the school. We headed back to Buckman's hotel.

"I want you to meet me at 7 a.m. instead of 6:30. This way Ed won't have to sit waiting such a long time, drawing attention from the soldiers and the tower," he said.

Once more, I steered my Volkswagen back down the highway to my motel on the outskirts of the city.

Before turning in, I once again organized my gear and documents as a doctor might prepare his medical bag for a house call. I had all the translated documents organized for the van drive, and then if we made it out, copies for U.S. customs. I had a change of clothing for Stephen since he would be wearing a school uniform. Street clothes would be less conspicuous, we figured. I had guessed at his sizes. I had also brought a few small toys from his room plus his favorite book that I used to read to him.

On the eve of the 470th day of Stephen's disappearance, I set two alarms to wake myself before daylight. As I began to reach for the light, I caught my own image in the mirror on the ceiling looking back at me in the bed. I studied my own eyes looking for support from within and again searching for clues as to why it had come to this.

"You have the courage to bring him home!" I reasoned, mouthing the words "courage."

BROKEN TREATY

BROKEN TREATY

CHAPTER 16

A STORM IS COMING

I headed out a little earlier than I needed to that morning so I could stop by the restaurant at Buckman's hotel. The restaurant hadn't opened yet, but I talked a waiter into getting me a glass of milk to try to calm my stomach. I drove on to meet Buckman at the rendezvous. Again, just like yesterday, he was waiting for me and met me at my window before I could turn the motor off. The look of concern on his face telegraphed that I was in for some more bleak news.

"Ed got a weather report last night from our guy in Brownsville. Forecast says a front is moving in off the gulf from the east. To beat it, the plane has to be in the air no later than 9 a.m., with or without us. Let's hope we're on it," Buckman said, his brow deeply furrowed.

"Everything is riding on this, Pat. It seems like not much more can go against us."

"If he doesn't show today, we'll keep trying even if we have to come back to Mexico," he offered.

That wasn't what I needed to hear, especially at this moment.

I followed him once more into town until I turned onto the street where we were to meet Mike, as we had done yesterday. He appeared in his white rented Topaz within minutes and promptly got behind the wheel of my VW. There was not much talk between us. I preferred it that way.

To keep Ed and the plane at the field another day I would have

BROKEN TREATY

tried to convince Pat to let me try to schmooze the field master. But the news of the Cherokee's forced evacuation left the fate of the rescue hanging in the next 30 minutes.

Just a few days before I arrived in Xalapa, my older brother Tommy called from El Paso, Texas.

"Steve," he explained over the phone, "Silvia's father, Alberto, may not be the sole reason that the cops would rob you and then 'disappear' you. They might look at the situation as the wealthy U.S. stepping all over Mexico, exploiting their poverty and thumbing our noses at them and their judicial system.

"If you get caught, bribe your way out within the first few minutes before the higher-ups get involved. The key words to use should be 'how can we take care of this matter'," he urged.

I hadn't mentioned this to the others. I didn't want to make anyone more nervous than they already were. Besides, I figured if it went bad—Pat had the resources to take care of Mike and the pilot.

We parked at the spot where we hoped to recover Stephen. The small horseshoe shaped street showed a little activity with pedestrians and cars heading to the boulevard at each end of the loop. We attracted no attention, although we must have looked out of place. Parents walked their children toward school. The sun made progress on the crisp morning shadows, beginning to heat the still air.

Mike showed off the new sunglasses he had bought. I had urged him to get his hands on a black leather jacket to be a little more convincing as some kind of official, but the best he could come up with was a black and white windbreaker.

"What do you think?" Mike asked as he put on the windbreaker and pushed the sunglasses up the bridge of his nose.

"You look like a tourist with sunglasses and a black and white windbreaker," I said, feeling it didn't much matter anymore.

His attempt to look official would have to do. I reminded myself that his role had unintentionally changed as well and that I should be grateful. I wore blue jeans and a green long sleeve heavy cotton shirt and tennis shoes to be able to move fast.

"I think the van is coming."

From his side mirror, Mike saw the black and yellow van pull onto our street and move toward us. The next few seconds would determine my fate as a father. Looking over my left shoulder through the rear window of my rental, I saw the van coming.

"Where's Pat? He's supposed to be in front of the van!" I said confused, yet somehow still calm. The van pulled up to the curb 20 yards in front of us and the driver gave two long blasts on the horn. At the same moment, Buckman paused in his Lincoln beside us, then moved ahead a few yards and stopped again. Mike and I looked at each other wondering if the other had seen a signal. We looked back again at Buckman and saw the signal, not simply a nod, but a fully extended arm, his finger pointing with great animation at the van.

Stephen was on the van!

Adrenaline rushed through my veins. "It's time to go home, Son," I said to myself as my hand automatically grasped the door handle. I believe I startled Mike at how fast I emerged from the car, saying nothing. I walked with an energy-charged pace as I neared the van. Mike had scrambled to catch up from behind me, though I wasn't aware of his movements.

BROKEN TREATY

Off to my right, I noticed a woman walking toward the van with a uniformed child in tow. We arrived at the van's side door at the same instant, but I thrust my arm out ahead of hers to grasp the door handle first. She submissively took a step back in an effort to understand my behavior as I opened the door.

I didn't pause to scan the faces of the dozen or so children crammed into the van, but saw that Stephen was sitting where we guessed he would be, in the seat closest to the door. As I swung my head toward the driver, I refrained from my first instinct to put my hands on his shoulders and comfort him. The importance of Buckman's instructions to be convincing as a Mexican officer served a purpose. The driver, a woman in her mid-30s, had turned to witness the commotion.

In a clinical, non-aggressive voice I said in Spanish: Good morning. We are here to recover a minor child by the name of Stephen Fenton. This is a copy of the Court Order from the State of Veracruz along with a copy of the Custody Order from The United States. Please continue on to the school and give these documents to the staff."

Before I could finish, the driver's mouth dropped, to let out a blood-curdling scream, sending a shockwave of panic through the children. I dropped the documents on the passenger seat next to the driver.

My head turned immediately from the driver to where Stephen sat closest to me. The other children watched with terror. There were about 10 children on board, between the ages of 6 and 7, all dressed in uniforms, white shirts, with dark green slacks for the boys and green plaid skirts for the few girls on board.

BROKEN TREATY

The children, I believe, must have thought we had come for them as well. I looked away from the sea of frightened faces, looking now down to meet the eyes of Stephen. I immediately recognized the fear in his eyes. He didn't recognize me. Obviously alarmed, he had heard his name mentioned during my instructions to the driver. His terror intensified as I turned now to lift him out of his seat.

"Stephen, this is Dad – it's time to go home, Son," I tried to reassure him.

My heart would have been broken if my instincts had not told me that he simply didn't know who I was. I thought I would be able to explain when I got him in the car. His face was pale and his eyes had dark circles under them, but aside from that he hadn't changed from how I remembered him. I lifted him from his seat, but I wasn't prepared for what happened next.

He still grasped a heavy backpack as I drew him closer to me. He kicked and screamed as I carried him walking toward my car. I repeated over and over "It's me, Dad, it's me, Dad." My young son wasn't hearing me. One of his shoes dropped to the ground. He knocked my glasses off, now revealing my blue eyes, as I began to open the front passenger door of my Volkswagen.

"Back seat!" Mike shouted. While Stephen continued struggling, I managed to get the rear door open and held Stephen tightly as I slid us both toward the middle of the rear seat.

Stephen had pulled a few fistfuls of hair out of my head and I saw the hair piling up in my lap as I now held him still struggling. "Stephen it's okay, it's me, Dad. I'm here to take you home!" It was useless. He only wanted to get away. The woman who had stepped back from the van with her child, stood frozen not believing what she was witnessing. I was only vaguely aware of others who had stopped to watch the disturbance.

Mike had trouble getting the engine to catch. It had stalled on me when cold but ran fine when warm. It had only been turned off for a few short minutes. I couldn't coach Mike on getting the engine while trying to calm Stephen. I was trying to restrain his arms to keep him from hurting himself. After several attempts the engine finally caught.

Instead of pulling around the stopped van to leave; Mike backed the car directly down the street toward the avenue where we had entered the loop. We rolled out backward onto the avenue, and upon incredible luck, into a brief break in traffic. Mike had a split second to throw the transmission into first gear and get us moving up the avenue, just as cars coming up on us had to slow down a bit as Mike wound through the gears.

At the crest of the hill we made a right. About 200 yards ahead we made another right turn. Stephen was still doing his best to break free. He punched, kicked and even tried squeezing my scrotum to loosen my grip. My hug around him only grew tighter as I worried that he might injure himself. He was as determined to escape as I was to hold onto him. He began to scream for help in Spanish. "Socorro! Ayuda!"—"Help me," he cried out. It suddenly occurred to me that maybe he'd forgotten English. I repeated in Spanish what I'd been saying in English, but he wasn't giving up the struggle. I saw no chance of calming him down before the car switch. We would have to move fast.

Mike steered the VW to the left curb on a dead-end street. We parked, and I lifted Stephen out of the car, still fighting me and yelling out for help. I saw Buckman coming toward us in his Lincoln. Twenty-five yards from us he turned his car around and stopped in the middle of the street. It was the most disturbing feeling, carrying a terrified child, screaming for his life "Help me. Help me!" I truly expected that a well meaning bystander would react to the horrific scene and intervene.

I was torn about the drama, but intuitively projected that if we could get through the initial terror triggered by the driver at the van, I could demonstrate or say something that would indicate that I was not a villain.

Why had Buckman stopped so far away from me? Running now, I moved toward the Lincoln, but the car moved away by the time I had come within six feet of the right side passenger door. I saw no sense in the action, and continued running toward the car now stopped another 20 yards ahead with Stephen still trying to pull away. Again, the Lincoln pulled away. I stopped. I could only hope that he would signal some kind of reasoning to the madness. My heart was racing.

Pausing, not knowing what else to do, I tried to catch my breath as I saw Pat turn around in his seat, pointing furiously behind me. What couldn't have been more than four minutes seemed an eternity. Anyone who had been walking now stood motionless in shock. Women held their hands over their mouths and men stared in disbelief while children watched, no one understanding why the gringos were trying to steal a child

Mike's white Topaz moved toward me from behind. I realized then that I was trying to get in the wrong car! Mike had locked up the keys to the VW and gone to his car with Stephen's backpack.

He pulled up beside me. Before he could stop I had the right rear door open and was sliding across the seat with Stephen firmly in my arms.

"Mike, I didn't realize we were to get into your car, I really screwed up." He was silent. His task at hand now was paramount – to drive. I watched the faces of the bystanders as we followed behind Buckman's Lincoln. I wanted some good distance from that street fast. There must have been 50 or 60 people, men, women and children, stopped dead in their tracks, watching our car move quickly down the end of the street. There we found ourselves stopped watching traffic speed past us. Right turns on red are illegal in Mexico.

Mike studied the traffic, looking for an opening. At this corner to my right, a Pemex gas station had all the pumps going with a line of cars four or five deep at each pump island. Now, at least a dozen people were giving their full attention to the commotion caused by a panicked 7-year-old in the white Topaz, who was nearly outwrestling me while screaming for his life.

A large man only a few feet from our car, wearing a white traditional Guayavera shirt, boldly stepped toward the Topaz and stretched out his hand in an attempt to open the door. Mike's hand came slapping down on the lock at the same instant. I hadn't realized that the door was unlocked. The large man removed his hand, backed away a few feet and studied the situation. Mike finally found a hole, or at least made one, in the traffic. We sped toward the center of the city. The green traffic signals were now many, stopping for only a few red lights. The intersections made us highly vulnerable to a run-in with an interested policeman or transit cop; commonplace downtown,

BROKEN TREATY

especially during rush hour.

Stephen continued his relentless determination to break free from me. I was amazed at his stamina and wondered how much longer he could keep it going; his adrenaline had at least matched mine. I continued to try to comfort him, now in Spanish as I considered he might have lost all of his English. He cursed me. The only English I heard from him was "Fucking-you!" he said in a heavy accent and then spit in my face.

My belief in what I was doing never wavered, but the drama convinced me that the time element was quite real. I began to fear that no matter the outcome, there would be some level of emotional wounds. If I could get him home, would the wounds eventually heal? I had the rest of my life as his father to help him heal. I stayed focused hanging onto Stephen, watching for police as we neared the edge of town, hoping that no one would try to follow.

I was able to manage Stephen to a seated position on the floor with my hands on his shoulders to keep him down, when Mike announced in a surprisingly calm manner, "there's a police car two cars behind us."

I trusted his eyes enough not to turn around to see for myself. I waited for his further description of what the cop was doing. I didn't believe that the cop had been alerted, but worried that he might have seen the commotion or heard Stephen's cries.

"He's turning left," Mike announced. The patrol car was out of sight by the time we moved through another intersection. Buckman's Lincoln was now just a few car lengths ahead of us, but we lost him as we came to another red light. Here we considered an option. We were at the head-of-the-line at the light. We could lose two or three minutes waiting for the light to change while no doubt drawing attention with Stephen in his terrified state. If we ran the light, we risked being pulled over. I scanned the street left and right. No traffic in either direction with no cops as far as I could see. We mutually decided to run the light. As we went through the intersection and headed down the avenue that led us away from downtown, we realized that the decision had been a good gamble as we were now the only car in sight and no one was pursuing us. Stephen continued his resistance.

The airfield was now only 15 minutes away and there was no sign that he was going to let up. There was no way we could get Stephen on the plane with a guard at the gate or passed the armed soldiers on the field if he wasn't going to go along with the rescue. A sobering thought raced through my head.

Buckman had asked back in California how I thought Stephen would react when he saw me. As close as I was to my son, I had rejected the notion that he would be anything but elated to see me; perhaps even a short lecture about taking so long to find him. Buckman had mentioned something yesterday as we considered other options to get Stephen out.

"Some of the children I've helped recover became panicked under the circumstances. In more cases than not, the abducting parent has told the child a story that would discourage them from asking about the other parent ranging from 'Mom doesn't love you anymore,' to 'your Daddy is dead.' Given the time that Stephen's mother has had him to herself, you can bet that she's told him something to put off questions about you, the father," Buckman cautioned.

As we raced down the highway, I spoke to Stephen in a gentle, but direct voice now in English. "Stephen, do you remember the time I took you camping, and when we were fishing you jumped in the lake, but didn't know how to swim and I pulled you out? Do you remember?" All at once the resistance left his body. A reckoning silence radiated from a heart and mind that recognized the voice of his father. At that moment, time had stopped. Now there was only Stephen and me, and the only real things that existed were the sounds of my voice and the hands that rested on his shoulders.

Waiting for an appropriate pause to let him absorb the impact of who I was, I spoke to him softly in Spanish: "Stephen, it's me, Dad, and I'm sorry it took me so long to come and finally bring you home. Do you remember how you cried for me to come and get you? I never gave up trying to find you. You're finally going home, Stephen," I said, eager for any response.

I could feel the confusion trying to process in his mind as he was still seated facing away from me, on the floor in front of my seat. In a sad, slow voice, he began to speak only in Spanish.

"Mom says you won't send her any money to take care of us," he said, his voice shaking.

"Son, listen carefully. I've spent all my time trying to find you and bring you home. Mom never had permission to keep you down here. I don't have time to explain everything right now, but I will as soon as we get on a plane that is waiting for us," I explained, giving him a few seconds to digest what I'd just said.

"Stephen, did you get a package with some Easter candy and gifts a couple of weeks ago?" I asked.

"Yes, but I don't know where it came from," he said.

"There was a small wooden airplane in the package. Did you get it?" I asked.

"Yes, it's in my room with my other toys. Did you send it?" he asked. He was progressively losing his apprehension.

"Stephen, that was my signal to you that I would be coming for you to take you home on a small plane just like the one I sent you. We're going home, Stephen, and I'm going to need your help so no one will try and stop us. Will you trust me until I can explain everything after we get on the plane?" I asked.

"Yes, Dad," he replied, seeming to accept the delicate significance of what lay ahead.

This was the most moving moment of my life. To figure I'd most likely abandoned him for nearly a year-and-a-half; my son had just granted me a fragile trust to get him to our freedom flight, perhaps in time to make it in the air before the field was shut down.

I could feel the tightness in his body begin to ease. His muscles relaxed. I offered him the seat next to me and he calmly climbed into it. He looked up at me and very curiously studied my face. I held back tears at the realization that I was now sitting and talking to my son, a son that I probably never would have seen again if I hadn't come to terms with the idea that this was the only way to get him home. I kept the positive dialogue going.

"Do you remember your bike? It's still at home waiting for you. I think one of the first things we can do is go for a bike ride like we used to." I suggested.

"That bike is too small for me now. I have a bike with five speeds," he proudly declared.

"Well, we'll have to see about getting a new bike for you when we get home," I told him.

BROKEN TREATY

With this incredible turning point, I saw that I just might be able to convince Buckman that we could get Stephen on the plane without creating a scene on the tarmac. A scene in front of the soldiers would certainly bring the rescue to a crash. Time was of the essence; every word counted.

"We need to walk across a runway to the plane, but there will be guards on the field who will want to stop us from flying home if you don't want to go." His big brown eyes opened wide, seeming to understand the importance of his role.

"Can you tell me now if you want to go and trust me?"

He replied, "Si!"—"Yes."

Minutes were critical, and I was sensitive to what had suddenly been imposed on him. The entire rescue implied that someone he loved so much had been incredibly deceitful.

I asked Stephen to change into the new grey shirt with green letters. He readily switched shirts. I showed him the new sweatshirt I brought in case he got cold on the flight and he approved. He had lost one shoe in the initial scuffle and this could be a problem, although his socks were dark green, at a distance, I hoped no one would notice they weren't shoes. I had no idea what shoe size he wore so I didn't bring shoes along. I had him take off his remaining shoe and I put it in my bag. I figured no shoes would be better than only one shoe.

We turned onto the highway that led to the airfield. I explained to Stephen that we would be climbing into the airplane through a rear door and I would show him where to sit and then buckle him in. I changed back and forth between English and Spanish trying to gauge his level at both languages.

BROKEN TREATY

"We're going home, Son, everything will be all right." I saw him studying my face again. I figured what he was thinking and beat him to his thoughts. I asked him in his new tongue. "You don't like the beard, do you? Don't worry. I'm going to shave it as soon as we get home. Would you like that?" He agreed with a nod.

A lot had transpired in just a few short minutes. We turned on to the highway that led south toward the airfield about 10 minutes away. The traffic was now nonexistent. I was only worried that Stephen might panic again when he saw the plane and have second thoughts about boarding, and draw attention from the soldiers. The future of three men lay in the hands of a 7-year-old boy.

Mike slowed the car and pulled onto the shoulder of the highway where Buckman's Lincoln had been waiting for us. Buckman began to transfer our bags to his trunk. I was surprised that we were doing another car switch. How had I missed all of this? Buckman asked how my son was doing. "He's okay now," I responded, as I lifted Stephen into my arms and walked toward the green Lincoln. At the front passenger window of Mike's car I thanked him sincerely. He was now taking off his watch and removing his sunglasses. He asked me to take his windbreaker and leave it in the Lincoln. I realized that Mike was trying to get rid of anything that might identify him as an accomplice.

"Good luck!" He said as I took the jacket from him. I carried Stephen and his heavy backpack to the rear seat of the Lincoln. With Stephen and me seated in the back, Buckman now pointed the sedan back toward the highway. Miraculously, no other cars had passed in either direction during the switch. This was the last leg of the drive, only a few miles from the field.

BROKEN TREATY

"Is Stephen ready for this?" Buckman asked, looking at my face in the rear view mirror to gauge the honesty of my response.

"Yes, Pat, I told him we're taking him home on a plane. He's pretty shaken up but he's given me his trust. We are good to go home!" I told him.

We slowed for the entrance to the field and soon approached the gate. A young security guard turned to our car, now stopped in front of the gate arm. I was nervous when he didn't give a friendly smile as I'd seen from him on Sunday. I wondered if there had been some buzz from the city. I looked to see if the securing strap was still buttoned across his revolver.

BROKEN TREATY

Chapter 17

Remembering life before Spanish

The guard watched our car for an awkward moment until oddly, he smiled, only now recognizing us. He waved as he stepped back into the guard house to punch the button that raised the gate. We proceeded through the gate waving and smiling back. Buckman hadn't said a word; demonstrating only calm since the last car switch, but now in a relaxed narrative, he began to give explicit instructions.

"When we stop, remove your bags from the car, pick up Stephen and begin walking directly to the plane," he instructed. "I'm going to disable the car but I'll be right behind you. Don't look back. Just act natural and hold Stephen's feet close to you so the soldiers can't see that he doesn't have any shoes."

The Cherokee stood about 100 yards from the Lincoln alone on the tarmac and clearly the only thing of interest on the field. No other aircraft was landing or taking off, nor another soul on the field, but for us and the soldiers. The control tower, close to the parking area, had full view of our movements. It was 8:20 now, well under the 9:00 a.m. "must fly" deadline.

The heat kept the soldiers in the shade away from the Cherokee. I saw only two of them back by the hangars and one near the entrance to the tower. I tucked Mike's windbreaker and Stephen's discarded shirt under the seat of the car and placed our bags on the ground. I gently lifted Stephen from the rear seat and held him in my right arm, perched on my hip, and leaned down to retrieve the bags.

I hadn't realized earlier how much heavier Stephen had become since I had last seen him. When I removed him from the van, he felt weightless as adrenaline rushed through me. I now realized that his body weight must have increased by 20 percent, a painful reminder of how long we'd been separated. No time to be angry, though. This was the happiest day of my life, rivaled only by witnessing his birth.

One hundred paces away was our escape flight. I didn't see Ed, though the canvas had been removed and the plane was untied with the pilot's door slightly ajar. I thought maybe he was somewhere nearby squabbling with soldiers over parking fees. My focus was to get Stephen across the tarmac and onto the plane without incident. Buckman had taken his bags out of the trunk and was now pulling an ignition part from the engine compartment of the Lincoln. I shifted my knees as I adjusted Stephen's weight and the bags I carried. I turned toward Buckman for his signal just as he slammed the hood of the Lincoln. He confirmed with a nod to move ahead. I began to take the most important steps of my life. At a field where there probably were no more than a few take-offs and landings a day, if any, the only thing to do was move ahead naturally under the nose of the soldiers and tower personnel.

I walked in a confident stride toward the white Cherokee with blue and green trim. I held Stephen close to me. I could think of nothing more calming to say than "I love you and I missed you so much."

He responded in Spanish "Te quiero tambien."—"I love you too."

The soldiers didn't move but simply watched us from the patch of shade cast by the buildings they guarded. The heat even at this

BROKEN TREATY

early hour was beginning to build. As we neared the plane, I saw Ed resting, behind the controls, completely unaware of our approach. Buckman followed 20 yards behind me, at a 7 o'clock position to try to obscure Stephen and me from the soldiers view.

"We're here, Ed," I called out. Our pilot sat up abruptly and turned to us.

"Let's get out of here. They keep asking if we're going to fly today," he said – his voice shaky.

"Let's go now, Ed, if this thing is ready to fly," said Buckman as he now walked up from behind.

I opened the left rear door of the plane and pointed out to Stephen where he would be sitting. I set him into the opening to crawl directly to his seat. I stowed our bags in back and took my seat, to find that Stephen had already buckled himself in. I was stunned at how relaxed and cooperative he had become in such a short time, especially after his initial reaction back at the school van. He now seemed to wholeheartedly accept the idea that we were going home. His mother had lied to him and hidden him from me and the authorities on both sides of the border. What she had done to him I would never forget, yet my heart shared how he must feel about leaving his mother so suddenly and the life he had come to know. I would tell him that I was certain his mother would be back in his life again soon after we got back home to California.

Buckman stowed his gear now climbing to his seat through the wing door as Ed brought avionics and radio gear to life, instinctively flipping a pattern of switches and rotating dials.

"How did it go?" Ed asked Buckman, as he adjusted his headset.

"They're probably looking for us by now. We'd better get off the

BROKEN TREATY

ground fast."

"I'm all over that...clear prop!" Ed yelled. The Lycoming 540/300 horsepower engine cranked a few quick turns before spinning to life. He idled for a moment adjusting the fuel mixture. Within 60 seconds Ed began guiding the plane toward the runway access road, pausing briefly at the runway entrance to wait for clearance from the tower. We all listened for anything from the overhead speaker that would indicate trouble. The tower transmissions were garbled and made worse by the incomprehensible attempt at English that crackled through the overhead cockpit speaker. Both Buckman and Ed looked at me to translate as noise came through the speaker.

"The guy is trying to speak English – your guess is as good as mine," I told them.

This went on two more times. Minutes were wasting. Ed told the tower we were taxiing to the runway and would report 10 miles out on course to Poza Rica. We didn't wait for a response.

It took a few minutes to get to the end of the runway and I kept watching the entrance hoping I wouldn't see a fleet of police cars streaming on to the field to head us off. We turned onto the runway holding area and Ed throttled the engine while holding down the toe brakes to get the "wiggles" out. Nothing was going to stop us. Normally we would have communicated with the tower to get barometric calibration for the altimeter. We didn't to minimize contact with the tower. Ed could calibrate the altimeter from the tower as we neared Brownsville, where accurate altitude would be more critical.

Ed wanted out of there just as bad as all of us, and not even an order from the tower or a blocked off runway was going to keep us on the ground.

"I'm just going to go for it and pretend we can't understand if they call us back," Ed reasoned. If someone tried to stop us, we'd try to fly below radar along the coast all the way to Brownsville. At 2,000 RPM, Ed released the toe brakes and we lunged forward. Ed rotated the yoke back at about 70 knots and the plane climbed at a steep ascent angle above the lifeless field. We all gave a tourist wave and smiles as we passed the sight line of the occupants in the tower. I made eye contact with the field master and the tower technician promoting a return good-bye wave. I watched the entrance to the airfield and the highway beyond for any activity to find the gate still and the highway empty in both directions.

The cockpit was quiet as we continued to climb. I turned my head toward Stephen, sitting inches to my right, looking out the window, studying the shrinking landmarks. Ed had filed a decoy flight plan to Poza Rica on another northern heading to help buy some time by confusing authorities in case anyone tried piecing together our actual flight plan.

Piloting the plane was virtually the same as when I'd been flying, but I could tell this Cherokee was the Cadillac of small planes, with a more than adequate power plant that could accommodate up to six passengers with proper weight distribution. Ed had state of the art avionics including GPS that was still under development when I was flying Cessnas, not seeing it in aviation use until now.

We followed a northeast heading as I began my assignment, listening to Spanish radio transmissions from the overhead speaker. I had to lean forward in my seat to listen carefully. At 10 miles out, Ed radioed our position and the tower acknowledged. After disappearing beyond some hills into a valley of tangled jungle that obscured the view of us from the tower and its radar, Ed turned off the plane's transponder eliminating our radar signature. We were running silent now. There would be no further communication from our plane. We all held our breath as Ed turned in the direction of our true heading—Brownsville, Texas, U.S.A.

I thought Ed would be at ease when we left the ground, but instead he became edgy and lost his sense of humor. From his perspective, getting off the ground was only the first step. I think that Buckman's comment about a search for us by now spooked Ed. He gave me the feeling that he still saw us as vulnerable and far from being untouchable.

I listened for any alarming transmissions that might concern our flight. Ed scanned several frequencies, which required fierce concentration on my part. At about 4,000 feet we did a slow banking turn, first left, then right to see if any aircraft might be coming up on us. We would repeat this maneuver every 15 minutes or so.

I was pretty damn sure we had made it after we were airborne. My instincts told me that we were home free even though we were still over 400 miles from the United States. I believed that they were still trying to sort things out in Xalapa.

"I'm not too sure about what the Mexican Air Force has in its fleet, but if some cowboy tries to force us down we might be able to get a distress call to the U.S. Coast Guard that might offer an escort," Ed told Buckman.

"Don't count on that kind of help for a couple of hours. We are nowhere near a Coast Guard base," Buckman said.

Given my task, I could only watch Stephen quietly studying the landscape and coastline ahead in the distance. I was desperate to console him and share what I'd brought from home with him.

The radio transmissions tapered off for a while. I tapped Buckman on the shoulder.

"Do you think the authorities are on to this yet?" I asked trying to be heard over the vibration of the engine.

Buckman craned his head around to look at me. Instead of speaking he gave me a very animated nod, indicating much more than words could depict. He was on high alert, scanning for other aircraft that might be interested in us.

The concern was that another plane would report our position and altitude as is routine. If air traffic control demanded us to identify ourselves, we weren't going to and that would raise suspicion. Soon, however, we'd be over international waters and it would be less of an issue, I told myself.

The two-bladed propeller pulling us ahead, sliced through the static air of the humid gulf-coast sky. A large gray wall of cloud bank loomed over the water many miles to the east, rising 20,000 feet or better. This must have been the front that required our plane to be in the air by 9:00 a.m.

Stephen had been very quiet, gazing out the window since takeoff. The struggle had exhausted him and it showed. Taking advantage of the quiet airwaves, I turned to Stephen and caught him looking up at me with his "island-size brown eyes." His face telegraphed a look of bewildered innocence. He could not fully understand all of this; perhaps grasping to remember a life before Spanish as he sat next to the father who had promised to bring him home a lifetime ago.

I lowered my head for him to see my scalp and asked him gently,

BROKEN TREATY

"Do I have any hair left on my head?" He had pulled several handfuls of hair out of my scalp during the drama.

He didn't answer but a shy smile crossed his face. I saw this as an opportunity to pull out some of his favorite things from his bedroom at home that I had thought to bring along. I put a small killer whale in his perfect hand. He was mesmerized as he carefully studied the stuffed toy. I continued asking him if he remembered each object as I introduced it into his hands. He answered "Si" with a look of surprise and smile of remembrance studying the reminders of home now piling up in his lap. A small Lego toy still preserved as he had built it; two racing cars from his slot track; a Batman; a Ninja Turtle figure, and a couple dozen favorite baseball cards he had skillfully traded for.

He grasped at the objects, trying to keep them in his lap as they began to fall to either side of his seat. I now showed him the photographs; pictures of the family and his cousins in California. I even had a picture of Stephen proudly holding a handsome string of trout we caught the day he fell in the lake on our fishing trip.

Before I could get any further, sharing the first meaningful moments with Stephen, Ed began barking at me to listen to the voices now squelching over the radio. Ed turned around, handing me a headset.

"Listen good, I want to know if anyone is looking for us or if we've been spotted!" He demanded sharply. I felt bad, turning my attention from Stephen who was still spellbound by the items from his bedroom.

I now translated everything that was coming over the radio to appease Ed. The usual back and forth chatter between tower and aircraft. Sometime later however, I heard something that compelled me to pull the headset tighter over my ears.

"I have an aircraft at 10,000 feet moving fast over the coast heading north," I translated. I listened intently for anything further regarding our description and position, but heard nothing more. Buckman studied my face as I continued to listen, looking for any signs that might indicate I was hearing more about us.

By now we were all scanning the sky for a dot that would be the aircraft that spotted us. Ed became even more alarmed, beginning lazy "S" turns again to get a good look around us. We saw only the sea and coastline far below, becoming obscured with thick haze in all directions from the encroaching low pressure front. For a good half hour I sat up in my seat scanning the sky for the dot that may have given away our position. I figured it had to be an aircraft passing below as it is more difficult to spot a plane against the backdrop of landscape than from above. I continued translating radio transmissions as they came over the headset. I thought it was pointless to translate everything but it made Ed feel better. I began to consider that no one had taken any further interest in us and it was just some well-meaning pilot trying to keep the airways safe by calling out the positions of other aircraft.

"If we were being pursued, chances are that further communications would have been restricted to frequencies that we couldn't access anyway, so there isn't much point in us getting too worried," Buckman said.

All I knew was that every revolution of the prop brought us a little closer to U.S. soil. The air seemed dramatically calm. In my earlier days while flying I seemed to experience nothing but turbulence, but

BROKEN TREATY

I'd never flown above 7,000 or 8,000 feet, so I figured that either the air was calmer at this higher altitude or that the stagnant and humid gulf coastal air made for passive flight.

As we neared the point of no return – an hour out of Brownsville, the intensity in the cockpit dissipated. Stephen had fallen asleep still clutching the reminders from home. I watched him as he slept. There is an innocence in a child's face when they sleep. Stephen always had a look about him when he slept that reminded me of him as an infant. To see him rest as I used to watch him, seemed surreal now. I had dreamt dozens of times about our reunion. Each time I awoke from that dream I would feel angry at myself for becoming so vulnerable to such a slim hope. Now here I was staring at my son and about to land on U.S. soil. Beyond recourse from Mexico (I thought), less than an hour from the greatest country on this globe, I was overcome with emotion and allowed myself to discreetly cry for both joy and sorrow. Joy for the rescue and recovery of my son and sorrow for him because of what his mother had done to create this scenario.

By now Ed and Buckman felt comfortable enough to let me remove the headset. The GPS indicator that was lashed to Ed's yoke continued to run off minutes remaining in flight. The haze grew thicker as we neared Texas and I began to understand the importance of the takeoff window that was explained when we met before the rescue that morning. A huge front was bearing in from the Gulf and we were just beating it.

During the final hour of our flight, I became concerned about a vibration in the engine that felt like misfiring. The misfire was slight but noticeable enough to cause me to scan the coast and guess where Ed might try to put down if we had to glide to a landing. I watched Ed and Buckman to see if they would glance at each other, indicating a valid concern. The two men remained silent and looked ahead. I watched to see if Ed might try to adjust the fuel mixture but he never did. I dismissed my worry and turned my attention again to Stephen who had been drifting in and out of sleep, but still clutched his things from home in his lap.

"Stephen, did you get any of the other packages I sent or any of my letters?" I asked.

"I got a few things someone sent, but Mom didn't tell me who they were from or give me any letters," he replied. He mentioned receiving a Jimmy Buffett cassette tape with our favorite songs that we played every morning on his way to school. He played it until it finally fell apart. It consoled me to know that he had access to something that reminded him of home and hopefully me.

Stephen's eyelids grew heavy again and I made him comfortable with a rolled up sweater for a pillow. He slept again for the rest of the flight. I looked around for a moment, taking in this entirely surreal scenario, beginning to feel the impact of what we had accomplished over such enormous odds. The grey storm front off the plane's starboard wing seemed to play with colors, making brown, green and grey dance around the cockpit adding a dreamlike dimension to the plane's small cabin.

So many things had gone wrong over the last three days that something had to finally go right. We were almost back in the U.S. with Stephen, giving me the opportunity to resume the terribly underrated honor of fatherhood. I was now penniless, but if one could measure fatherhood in terms of prosperity, I was a very

BROKEN TREATY

wealthy man.

Ed started to power up navigation essentials; flipping switches in intricate sequence to revive avionics, the radio transmitter and plane's transponder, indicating he no longer saw a danger from Mexican airspace. We began drifting back toward Mexico, to eliminate confusion to U.S. authorities about our flight's origin. We would enter the U.S. from Mexico--not from the Gulf.

I gently woke Stephen from a solid sleep and pointed through the Plexiglass windshield as the panorama of Brownsville, Texas, filled our cockpit view.

"In just a few minutes we'll be landing in the United States," I explained in Spanish.

"We'll be going through customs here and then if we can find a flight right away, we'll be on a long flight back home to San Francisco, maybe even making it back tonight."

We were now flying across the border into the U.S., while Ed took instructions from Brownsville tower for landing.

I was excited, proud, happy and incredibly relieved. We had made it. I wanted to shout and cheer but I restrained myself; I realized it wasn't fair to Stephen to celebrate after what he'd endured only three hours earlier.

I pointed out the airport to him as the Cherokee lined up for final approach. Descending slowly from the thick graying sky, none of us, not even Pat Buckman could have envisioned what was in store for us in Brownsville.

BROKEN TREATY

Steve and Stephen after landing in Brownsville.
The FBI was on the way.

Chapter 18

The FBI Arrives

As we dropped gently onto the runway in Brownsville, I exhaled a deep breath I hadn't been aware I was holding. We'd been lucky and no one knew that better than I. Stephen smiled up at me with an eager gaze, seemingly trustful about our next adventure. I explained to him that we'd be going through customs and would then catch a flight on a bigger plane to Houston. I didn't know if we would be able to get a flight right out to San Francisco or whether we'd need to spend the night. I didn't really care, but I knew my family, ready to throw their arms around Stephen, would. We were both still numb and somewhat subdued as we climbed out of the plane. Buckman stood in front of us holding a camera, offering to take a photo.

"You bet," I responded, knowing it would be one I would treasure for life. The air was hot and muggy. I was still wearing the dark long-sleeve shirt I had put on at sunrise, but I was happy to be sweating because of the heat and no longer from the drama. After two shutter releases Pat approached.

"I have found that it's best after a rescue, that I part as soon as possible so that I'm not a constant reminder of what the child has just been through. It will give you both a chance to be alone and start adjusting to each other. I will be gone as soon as we get your son through Immigration."

His disclosure was abrupt, but high in logic. I put out my hand, unable to find the suitable words to thank him.

BROKEN TREATY

"Just be good to your son and keep a sharp eye on him," he said.

Ed neared us. "I hope we never have to meet again," he said with a smile – the first I believe he'd ever shown. "Take care of your son." I realized what he had risked and was grateful.

We now made our way toward the customs office. Inside, an immigration official and a customs officer were busy reviewing the documents of a group of men in suits obviously just returning from a business trip across the border. Buckman submitted my paperwork along with Stephen's for their inspection while I took a seat with Stephen in a small row of chairs a few feet away. The two officials never looked up as they reviewed our birth certificates and my custody order. I had anticipated something of a routine challenge as to the validity of my documents, especially in light of the fact that Stephen was shoeless. It occurred to me that if anybody began questioning him, they had better speak Spanish, not great proof that he was my son. Buckman soon returned with our documents.

"We're all set," he said, handing me the paperwork. I was a little surprised at how casual the whole process had been. I would have figured that any one returning from Mexico on a private plane would fall under terrific scrutiny. I had become cynical about the dynamics of any official entity. As of this moment I no longer had a legal struggle or diplomatic challenge. I looked forward to getting beyond my paranoia. Only good things were ahead for Stephen and me.

A stranger approached me as Stephen and I moved through a corridor toward the entrance to the terminal. My heart skipped a beat. Why was this stranger about to speak to me? I wondered. He stopped, smiled and extended his right hand.

"Congratulations on getting your son home" he said, cheerfully.

BROKEN TREATY

The man had wavy blond hair and a British accent. The only logical explanation was that the man was the source feeding weather information to Ed in Xalapa about the storm front. I hadn't heard mention of the blond stranger, but there was likely much that served no purpose for me to know. We chatted briefly about the flight and then I shook his hand, thanking him as we parted. My heart slowed, and I chided myself for being paranoid.

I led Stephen by the hand through the doors to the terminal. I was struggling with the three bags, so when Stephen offered to carry his back pack, I handed him the heavy bag to see how he would handle it. I realized as I did so that I should have been carrying him – he was walking through the terminal in his socks – but I figured the task was a good distraction for him. He hoisted the weighted bag over his right shoulder. The officials in immigration had no interest in our baggage, which might have cleared the mystery of the weight.

I grinned asking, "what could possibly be so heavy in your back pack?"

"Libros," he replied. His mischievous grin only indicated a half-truth.

While the weight of the sack slowed Stephen's pace, I floated along, tethered by his hand. I was the luckiest man on the planet and I couldn't wait to share the news with everyone I knew.

We found the United Airlines ticket counter and were getting squared away for a flight to Houston and a connection on to San Francisco. We'd be home that night. Buckman approached asking a small favor.

"Could you call the rental-car place back at the airport in Veracruz for me? I need to tell them where they can find the Lincoln and that the coil wire is in the glove box," he said.

I found a bank of phones, and made the call for him, though my explanation to the man at the rental desk in Veracruz was dubious about my details, believing I was a lunatic and sarcastically dictated a list of outrageously inflated surcharges for the recovery of the Lincoln. I decided to wait until I got home to handle my issue with the Volkswagen I had abandoned.

Now I made the most important call of all--to my parents. I knew my family was anxious for word about whether we'd made it. The last message from me was desperate and bleak. For all they knew, the rescue had been a failure. I punched the number and my dad picked up. My voice cracked as I said, "Dad, I'm in Brownsville."

A pause followed and then the words from a very emotional grandfather, "My God," he said.

"Dad, there's someone I'd like you to talk to," I said as I passed the phone to Stephen. Stephen's face lit up when he recognized the word "Grandpa," and he took the phone from my hand.

"Hola, Grandpa," Stephen said through the phone. He was ecstatic to hear another important voice from the past. I could hear the excitement through the receiver from my father as the two struggled to understand each other. Grandpa did most of the talking, but Stephen seemed to be following some of the dialogue as the two were ecstatic at being able to talk again. Dad put my mom on, and I imagined the smile on her face as she heard Stephen's voice for the first time in 16 months.

The conversation was brief, and soon Stephen handed the phone back to me. I didn't go into the drama of the rescue with my parents. I would do that later, when the time was right. After giving my dad

BROKEN TREATY

the flight information, I hung up the phone with the reassurance that there would be quite a welcome for us in San Francisco. I hoped Stephen would see how deeply he'd been missed.

It was surreal to be walking hand in hand with my son, responsible for him once again. It felt good to be alive. Much of my livelihood had been drawn and quartered with the long progression of failures over the last 16 months. I had a new outlook and renewed hope in mankind, though my reconciliation had been self induced.

With a little time before our flight to Houston, I wanted to see if we could get a taxi into town to find some shoes for Stephen, knowing it would restore some dignity as he'd endured the homecoming thus far shoeless.

Before leaving the bank of telephones, I made one last call to the Vanished Children's Alliance back in San Jose. They put me on speaker phone with the staff gathered around. They cheered as I informed them we'd finally brought Stephen out of Mexico. They were eager to see both of us as soon as possible, and thrilled that they could now close his file. Still grinning, I placed the receiver back into its cradle and turned to find a house-sized customs officer standing behind me.

The seriousness of his issue was evident. He had his hand on the revolver at his side with the strap unsnapped, and a fierce, almost personal scowl on his face as he glared down at me. In that instant I realized that the rescue had drawn a hell of a lot more attention than any of us could have guessed. I had a very bad feeling.

"Is this your son?" the customs man asked, pointing to Stephen, who was by now shouldering his back pack.

"Yes, I've just brought him out of Mexico. He's been missing for

BROKEN TREATY

almost a year and a half," I tried to explain. The officer didn't seem interested in my story. He asked if I had any documentation for my son. Beginning to sweat again, I quickly produced a package of documents that I hoped would get us out of more trouble than the rescue might get us into. I showed him a copy of my certified custody order and Stephen's birth certificate. He glanced over them too quickly to absorb any content.

"Do you have any weapons on you?" the giant customs man asked.

"Of course not," I assured.

Everything began happening too fast for me to reasonably process. I was no longer in control. He put a hand firmly on my shoulder and walked me over to a vacant ticket counter while still clutching his holstered revolver. Stephen could only stand silently as he watched; nothing made much sense to him today. I felt my heart pounding as my mind raced. I had to convince him to release us.

Our activity began to draw the attention of onlookers at the busy terminal. At the counter he had me spread my hands and feet and commenced with a weapons search. I couldn't look at the faces of the bystanders who had stopped to witness the excitement. My only thought was of how I must look to my son, being treated like some kind or thief or smuggler in front of the gathering crowd. When the customs officer finished searching he turned me around.

"If you cooperate, I won't handcuff you in front of your son," he said.

"I won't be a problem. Can I carry my son?" I pleaded.

"The security guard will take care of your son," he answered and turned me in the direction of the customs office. I looked back to see

BROKEN TREATY

the security guard now speaking in Spanish with Stephen.

I kept my chin up as the customs officer escorted me ahead with a finger grasped around my rear belt loop. I turned my head around to see Stephen now walking with the guard about 20 feet behind me. I felt the shame in his heart watching his father being led off like a criminal. I tried to offer some reassurance. The worst thing I could do was let Stephen see me panic.

"Don't worry Son, it's just a mistake. They're going to ask us some questions and then let us get on the plane." His fragile trust was being compromised, but he was either very noble or just too confused as he walked behind, indifferent to the shocked faces of the onlookers.

To my left, I caught a glimpse of Buckman, stopped, with his mouth dropped open and eyes wide in disbelief; completely helpless. Because of his recent involvement, the best thing for all of us was for him to get out of Brownsville before anyone connected him to us. After the split-second eye contact I turned away from him knowing he'd contact the right person. I'd be on my own, but I still felt confident that the documents I carried would quickly clear up any confusion. I was hopeful we could still catch our flight to Houston. I kept turning around to comfort Stephen and try to reassure him, that it would all be okay. The 20-foot distance the customs officer and the security guard kept us apart seemed intentional, and I began to worry that they might separate us.

The customs man wouldn't tell me much, but he did indicate that I wasn't being arrested – only detained until two FBI special agents arrived to ask me some questions. I was doing all I could to keep my cool.

BROKEN TREATY

Stephen and I were led back into the customs and immigration area. I was taken to a small office directly behind the very same counter where our documents had been reviewed only a half hour before. As I was escorted through the door, I realized Stephen wasn't behind me. I began to panic.

My heart pulsed even faster and I clenched my fists in anger. I had been extremely cooperative to this point, but now I felt compelled to protest the separation between Stephen and myself. I could see Stephen through a window, sitting with the guard in the waiting area. I felt caged, and began pacing. I studied my surroundings and looked around for something small, but heavy. The customs officer assured me that Stephen would remain where he was until the FBI agents had talked to me.

I was asked to sit in a chair in the corner as a second customs officer joined us. The two men began to rummage through my bags. When they didn't find what they were after, the smaller second customs man turned as if this had become personal, just short of threats.

"We're going to search that plane. Are we going to find any weapons on it?" He demanded.

I looked purposefully into his eyes and answered in a steady, firm voice, "Absolutely not! Please feel free to search the plane. You just searched everything that I had on the plane!"

He seemed almost annoyed that I had nothing to hide.

The questions continued: Was the plane mine? Did I fly the plane? How many were on it? What were their names? I answered all but the last question. When I said I couldn't give their names, an odd thing occurred. I had expected him to become more aggressive through intimidation. Instead he asked in a gentler voice if they were friends.

BROKEN TREATY

This was a slow pitch. I nodded, and he stopped asking questions. He asked me to explain the situation. A small degree of relief came over me, being offered a chance to describe my 16-month ordeal and how I got Stephen out of Mexico that morning.

By the end of my story the large customs man had softened up a bit and offered some hope. He said that if my story checked out and that if my custody order and birth certificate were real, I would probably be released.

"But it's not up to us, it will be up to the FBI," he finished.

The officer allowed me to walk around the little office. I was able to look out to where Stephen was entertaining the security guard with the Batman toy he must have carried from the plane in his pocket. I was left to my own devices while waiting for the FBI, though not permitted to leave the room or have any contact with Stephen. I was offered some food from a party tray, but I couldn't eat. I asked if Stephen could come get some food, but they explained that he had been given some snacks and a Coke from a vending machine. I looked again through the glass. Stephen was enjoying his snack, still amusing the guard at his side. I realized that the glass was mirrored in one direction and that Stephen couldn't see me at all. This upset me, and I wondered again how bad today was going to get.

Two new faces, one Caucasian and one Latino, both in suits, arrived at the counter outside the window, and I figured these were the FBI agents. They chatted for some time with the first customs officer, occasionally looking in my direction and nodding to each other. The two men now entered the room where I was being held. They were surprisingly young. I put them at around my age; in their early to mid thirties. Special Agent Miles Hutchins extended his

BROKEN TREATY

hand and introduced himself and his partner. Special Agent Freddy Vela was less sociable and stood back a bit. I dug down deep to produce a slight smile as I gave Hutchins a firm handshake. I was hoping my openness would dispel any thoughts of my being a true offender.

Hutchins was eager to hear my story. I gave him some of the highlights of my endeavor to bring Stephen home under the terms of the Hague Treaty between the U.S. and Mexico. I was permitted to go through my packet of documents to find only a Spanish summary detailing my legal struggle with the Mexican government. Hutchins said it was okay because he read and spoke fluent Spanish. He read the documents with interest, and after putting the papers down he looked directly at me and began to explain why I was being held. He proceeded in a very clinical, almost sterilized voice.

"The Mexican government is charging you with kidnapping your son. They claim you assaulted a school bus with automatic weapons and that some shots were fired. They say you presented false documents and threatened the driver. They allege that you either stole, high-jacked, or commandeered an airplane and illegally took your son out of Mexico. The Mexican government maintains that the boy was born in Mexico and that he has a Mexican birth certificate. They have sent an official, from the Mexican Consulate here in Brownsville, to take the boy back. We're thinking about sending him back to Mexico," the agent concluded.

I stood staring at the special agent in disbelief, unable to assemble a response.

Chapter 19

Melanie Headrick's call

I turned to look through the glass only to see a new figure asking questions of my son. He was undoubtedly the consulate official – well dressed in a dark business suit and carefully groomed. There was an almost slick-salesman aura about him that troubled me. He had a pompous look in his eyes suggesting he considered it only a simple formality to take Stephen back to Mexico.

I thought about how my own government hadn't been much help in getting Stephen home. It was sickening to see now they wouldn't hesitate to let him be sent back. I felt enraged, panicked, and scared at the same time. My fury got the best of me, and I began pacing the perimeter of the tiny office uncertain that I could keep my sanity.

"I can't go through this again," I said desperately to Hutchins. "If my son is sent back to Mexico, I'll never see him again and you know it!"

"You shouldn't have done it this way," Hutchins responded. I turned to him, and took a seat directly in front of him to face him in his chair.

"Mr. Hutchins," I began, "if this was your child and you had no other way to ever see him again, what would you have done?" I waited for a reply, but there wasn't one. Instead, he looked down at his hands and changed the subject.

"It's not up to me. Right now, the Mexican Foreign Ministry wants a child back that they claim belongs to them. The State Department is no longer your friend. The U.S. Attorney's office in Washington will decide what will happen with your son," Hutchins warned.

Hutchins then asked for copies of my custody order and Stephen's birth certificate. I handed them to him, along with a copy of the Mexican pickup order that I'd given to the driver of the school van. These orders were the same orders generated from Mexico City to recover Stephen from Alberto's house.

"Where did you get this?" he asked, somewhat astonished. He seemed surprised that I would have had access to this document.

"The Mexican Central Authority faxed it to me on my request." I answered.

Hutchins read the order but said it only authorized the local authorities to recover my son. I pointed out that the purpose of recovering the child was to turn him over to me, so I could take him back home to California.

"The order still stood, the problem was getting the local authorities to execute it. Each time an attempt was made, my wife produced a custody order issued by a Mexican judge who was unaware of the Hague proceedings, and each time it took two to three months to have that order rescinded. Then it would take another month or two to send a local judge and police officer again to the house for another attempt," I explained. I paused for a moment, encouraged to see Hutchins growing more interested in my story.

I continued, "The Mexican Central Authority repeatedly denied my requests to accompany the Mexican authorities to get Stephen. They didn't even want me in the country until they had recovered him. I knew a rescue wouldn't be pleasant for my son, but do you think it would have been any less traumatic having perfect strangers

BROKEN TREATY

pick him up and hold him until I could arrive in Mexico City?" I challenged.

Hutchins looked a little overwhelmed by my revelations. If Stephen was taken from me now and sent back to Mexico, I wanted to make this personal to him.

"Now, I'd like to make a call," I demanded.

I felt as though I could have the whole thing cleared up in no time if I could get the right people talking to each other. My earlier requests to use the phone had been denied as the customs officer explained that there was only one line and they needed to keep it open. He told me I'd be given another opportunity later.

"Your call is going to have to wait. Every time that phone is hung up, it rings right away with another call regarding this case," he responded.

Through the picture window I now saw the Mexican Consulate official talking again with Stephen. "Hey, I don't want that guy near my son. He's only going to upset Stephen," I objected.

"He has diplomatic immunity. He can go anywhere and talk to anyone he wants and we can't do a thing about it," Hutchins said.

I continued to watch the interaction between the Mexican official and Stephen. I felt totally helpless and frustrated, confined in the small room, barred from Stephen and freedom. I resisted the urge to charge out of the room and demand the removal of the consulate official. Maybe a bad move that would probably work against me in the long run, I considered.

Both FBI agents abruptly left the small room. Hutchins began talking with the Mexican consulate official as Vela got on the phone. I believed I'd raised some doubts in Hutchin's mind as to the credibility of the Mexican government's claims. I overheard Vela on the phone saying to someone that they were trying to have an FBI agent in San Jose, California, personally verify my custody order and Stephen's birth certificate, but it would take time. The fact that there was only one phone line in this office, while the customs and immigration officers had to use the same phone for their business meant I'd be here a while, if I was ever to leave with Stephen at all. The whole thing had turned into an international incident and was getting more complicated by the minute.

I paced back and forth in the small office, watching and waiting, hoping for someone to call on my behalf who could add credence to my story. Telephone calls were continuous, and I could see that the customs and immigration people were becoming annoyed with the FBI agents who had commandeered their only telephone line.

Abruptly, Hutchins stuck his head in the doorway.

"I want to know if there are any guns on that plane?" he asked sharply.

"There are no guns," I responded, irritated. "Why don't you just search the plane?" I wondered why they kept asking me this. I could only figure that since we had already cleared customs, a warrant would now have to be obtained in order to search the plane. There were no guns.

Hutchins went on. "Mexican officials in Veracruz faxed over a copy of an order awarding custody to your wife, dated August, 1993," he told me.

"Yes, and if there were a reliable way to check it out, you would find that order, along with all subsequent orders has been defeated through and by the Mexican courts at local, state and federal levels.

BROKEN TREATY

Mr. Hutchins, my wife's custody order isn't valid. If I can just make a phone call, I can have Melanie Headrick, an investigator with the Santa Clara County District Attorney's office, verify my story." I pleaded. Hutchins couldn't look me in the eye as he responded.

"We're talking with the U.S. Attorney's office to see if we should send your son back; it'll be up to them. You'll get a chance to make your call later," he told me. He left the room.

I stared after him, feeling a despair I'd never known.

I was left alone for a long time. What seemed like hours later, agent Vela appeared with a copy of my custody order from February, 1993. He asked if the court's contact information was on the first page. I affirmed that it was, and he picked up the phone and dialed. He paused, said something into the phone and then gave me a confused look. Incredibly, he said that my father was on the line. I took advantage of the confusion and grabbed the phone out of his hand. He had inadvertently called my parents' house phone, which was also listed on the first page of the custody order, next to the court information. I would only have seconds before Vela would take the phone from me—I needed to make my words count.

"Dad, I'm being held by the FBI here in Brownsville. They say that they might send Stephen back to Mexico because of a bunch of phony allegations. You need to reach Melanie Headrick, then the State Department office in Washington and Diane Feinstein's office in Sacramento," I told him.

I didn't have to impress on him the urgency. My dad understood fully, and I knew he'd begin contacting these people as soon as we hung up. I felt a surge of hope as I pointed out the court house telephone number Vela had originally intended to dial.

BROKEN TREATY

By now Stephen and I had been detained over two hours, and our flight to Houston was long gone. The phone was in constant use. Communications were short, and each time the phone was hung up, it rang again instantly. The office door had been left open, and I sat near it, trying to follow developments where Vela was talking with another customs agent. Hutchins, who was on the phone, saw me trying to listen in, rolled his eyes and walked over to shut the door.

I went back to the window to look for Stephen, but he was no longer in the small waiting area in front of the counter. I feared he'd already been taken from me.

I panicked, beginning to yell, "Where is Stephen, where is my Son?"

The larger customs officer, using the computer in the room with me, calmly pointed through the window to a far corner where Stephen and the security guard were listening to the Mexican Consulate official. Stephen swung on a low gate while the official talked to him. It wasn't a stretch to figure what was going on. He was trying to get Stephen to ask to go back to Mexico, and he had plenty of time to work on him.

More time passed. Hutchins and Vela took turns making and taking calls. Hutchins popped his head in again. I had a lot of questions but he evaded them all, saying only that he was waiting for a call from the U.S. Attorney's Office to get approval to release me. I looked up, feeling some hope that the call might actually come.

"Have you gotten any calls on my behalf?"

"Yes. Probably 30 or more calls on your behalf—so many that we can't keep the line open to get the important ones," he confessed.

BROKEN TREATY

He offered no details. Hutchins wondered with irony if the phone had been so busy that the U.S. Attorney's Office hadn't been able to get through. I took on a little guarded optimism at this point.

It was closing in on four long hours that we had been detained, separated the entire time from Stephen. He could not see me through the mirrored window. I wondered what was going through his head. The treatment was brutal for both of us. I ached to hold him and reassure him that we'd be okay and on our way.

I had no idea where this was headed. If Stephen was going to be sent back to Mexico, undoubtedly I would be the last to know. There weren't enough federal agents from any branch in this airport to contain me if I saw the consulate official leaving with Stephen.

Finally, Hutchins came in. He had a relaxed look on his face.

"We've had all of your documents verified, including the arrest warrant for your wife. We've explained to the Mexican government that because your custody order was awarded six months prior to hers, we have no grounds to hold you," he said.

Special Agent Hutchins, moved closer to me for a private comment, before I could fully absorb the meaning of what he'd just explained.

"It seems you have someone looking after you. Headrick, the investigator back in San Jose, learned that we might be sending your son back to Mexico and she became livid. She told Vela and me, if that happened, it would probably be the last mistake of our career. She faxed over a copy of the warrant for your wife. She basically saved your ass. The State Department is furious with you and didn't really care if we sent your boy back."

Relief rushed over me. I could feel my eyes welling up.

BROKEN TREATY

"We'll bring you to your son, and then you're free to leave," he added.

"One thing," I said, pointing toward Stephen through the one-way mirror. "I'd like that consulate official escorted out of the airport. I don't trust that guy—he's bad news. He's had too much time to get into Stephen's head and mess with him," I pleaded.

I should have been elated with the news of our release, but I didn't know what other offended entity waited outside the customs office. I feared the Mexican government might try some other ploy to keep Stephen and me in Brownsville. Once we were freed by the FBI, I wouldn't be comfortable until we were on a big jet heading anywhere as long as it was north.

"Hutchins, can you hang around until we get on another flight? I'm worried that the Mexicans won't stop with you guys!" I asked. I thought it was the least they could do after what they'd put us through over the last four hours.

"We can't do that. Vela and I need to get back," he told me.

I was led into the outer office and noticed the frightened look on Stephen's face. I don't know why the consulate official hadn't been chased off with a big stick, but he was still there standing behind Stephen. Momentarily, I forgot my worries and broke into a big smile, and knelt down in front of him. "Everything is going to be okay now, Stephen," I said softly in Spanish. "We'll be getting on another plane in just a little while."

Stephen didn't return my smile. Instead, he began to cry and backed away from me.

"I don't want to speak English. I only want to speak Spanish," he sobbed.

BROKEN TREATY

I tried to tell him in Spanish it was okay, he could speak Spanish if he preferred, but he wasn't listening. Hutchins joined in, trying to reinforce what I was telling him.

"Mom says that you won't send us any money," he said. The same words he spoke when he realized who I was earlier that morning in the car. I chose my next words carefully.

"Stephen, your mom is not a bad person; she just made a bad decision by hiding you from me. It's time to go home Son," I tried to assure him.

He was in tears now and visibly upset. I moved slowly toward him and tenderly lifted him into my arms. He accepted my grasp by putting both arms around my neck. He seemed so small, so frail and broken; I couldn't help losing my temper. I turned toward the Mexican official and shouted in his own tongue: "Que has dicho a mi hijo, cabron"—"What have you said to my son, you son-of-a-bitch." I envisioned taking him into the parking lot to make an oil-slick out of him. The man had started backing up when Hutchins and Vela stepped between us and held me back. Vela took me, still carrying Stephen, back into the small room. Hutchins talked with the consulate official outside, while Vela urged me to calm down. Miraculously, as soon as the consulate officer was out of the room, Stephen began to relax in my arms and within minutes seemed to regain trust in me.

Almost immediately the large customs agent opened the door and told Vela that the Brownsville D.A.'s office was on the phone and wanted to talk to one of the FBI agents. My stomach knotted up again as Vela took the call. Vela listened for a minute then interrupted whoever was speaking.

BROKEN TREATY

"Do you guys know that the father has a custody order for his son from California?" he asked. "Well, I think you might want to look into that, because we're letting Fenton and his son, go." Vela put the phone down then turned to me with a perplexed look.

"You must have really pissed-off Mexico City. The Mexican consulate has retained an attorney who has rallied the D.A.'s office here in Brownsville to charge you with kidnapping. My advice to you is to get out of Brownsville as fast as you can," Vela told me.

I looked from the office toward where Hutchins had been talking to the Mexican official; neither was in sight. I expected to be arrested by the local police as soon as we emerged from the customs area into the airport lobby. I picked up our bags and held Stephen by the hand. Before I cleared the doorway, I turned to Vela. "Thanks," for what, I wasn't sure. He nodded to accept my gesture. I held my breath as we walked through the doors and into the airport lobby with Stephen.

Once through, I found Hutchins standing 50 feet away with his hands on his hips, in front of an exit. By the look on his face, I knew he had just escorted the Mexican consul through that exit. Nothing was said, but he gave me a look that I took to mean the Mexican consulate official wouldn't be bothering us anymore. As Stephen and I crossed the lobby I turned around several times to see if he was still there. He was.

The ticket agent at the counter gave me a nervous smile as I explained that I had missed my earlier flight. Obviously, this guy had the scoop on what was going on. He took my tickets and began processing them.

"There's another flight leaving in just a few minutes," he said.

BROKEN TREATY

"You still have time to board." Perfect," I thought. A call to my parents would have to wait. I couldn't get us out of Brownsville fast enough.

I grabbed our tickets and walked with Stephen the remaining steps to the gate and set my bags on the X-ray belt. I looked back toward Hutchins and saw he was gone. But I did see the security guard who had been with Stephen running toward us.

"Christ Almighty! – what now?" I groaned in disbelief. The guard reached Stephen and explained that he'd left something behind. He handed Stephen the Batman figure he had been playing with. Things aren't always what they appeared. We both thanked him and we were guided through the metal detector.

A strange feeling came over me as I collected our bags. I looked up to see at least five uniformed guards on either side of the departure gate with their eyes fixed on us. The way they were watching us, some standing, some sitting, I felt certain that one of them would step forward to start a new problem all over again. Stephen and I walked silently by them and onto the plane. We found our seats and stowed our bags. I put the bag with Stephen's toys from home at my feet. I never learned why the airport security had been so interested in us, or who had sent them. The only thing I could conclude was that a rumor circulated that I might have a weapon with me.

Even though we were on the plane, preparing for take-off, I couldn't relax, knowing the police might still detain us before we left the ground. I held out hope that Vela's words with the D.A.'s office would have them reconsider the charges. I struggled to gain control of my paranoia. I knew that whatever happened now was beyond my control. I'd done my best.

BROKEN TREATY

Once again, I tried to reassure Stephen.

"Son, I'm sorry for all that crazy confusion, but I think we're through the worst of it now." I knew that if I was detained again, I would eventually be released. This had been a compressed acid test, but it was the added trauma to Stephen that I wanted to avoid.

Not soon enough for me, the plane taxied to the runway and surged skyward.

Chapter 20

Homecoming!

As the big DC-10 left Brownsville and the Mexican frontier just beyond the runway behind, I allowed myself some optimism. Anywhere was going to be a better place than a border town. But the events that had taken place over the last seven hours hadn't begun to sink in. I realized I'd had little chance for any meaningful dialogue with Stephen. Up until this moment I had been managing our movements with instructions. The flight would be brief, but we had a little time to talk on our way to Houston. I didn't know if we'd have to roll with another round of punches there, or if he'd be taken from me for good, but I wanted to let him know that everything would be okay.

"Stephen, we'll see if we can find you a pair of shoes in the airport where we're headed, maybe even a pair of cowboy boots if we have time."

"Thank you," he responded softly.

"I have a copy of the small wooden plane that I sent you in the Easter package." I pulled the toy from my bag at our feet and placed it into his hands.

"Dad, this is the same plane from the package they gave me. It's the same plane I have in my room," he exclaimed, excited by the exact replica he now held in his hand.

I realized that he had been given the Easter package but not told of its origin. The little plane was a hand-carved single-engine wooden plane. I bought two of them – one to try to send to him and one for this very moment.

"I sent it to you as a secret signal that I would keep my promise to bring you home, and this was how we would be getting back. I was lucky enough to find some people to help us, like Pat Buckman and Ed, our pilot."

I could see from his reactions that Stephen was beginning to realize that dad hadn't just awakened one morning and decided to bring him home. He was realizing that a tremendous amount of planning had gone into his rescue. I knew questions were bound to come but I planned to respond carefully, avoiding any derogatory references to his mother.

I stared down at the dark brown backpack that was so heavy. "Stephen," I said in Spanish, "I just have to ask, what is so heavy in your bag? It can't be just books." He looked back up at me with a grin.

"Monedas!"—"coins!" he replied. He leaned forward and unzipped a hidden compartment in the backpack as a banker might open a vault. I looked down at the sack stenciled with "Banco de Mexico" that was filled with an array of coinage packed so tightly that the stitching was compromised.

"Whose money is it?" I asked.

"It's mine. I earned it working for Grandpa Alberto." I considered that Stephen's struggle during the rescue might have become more personal if I had not grabbed his backpack as I lifted him from the van that morning.

Alberto owned and ran four tortillerias in Xalapa, with one adjacent to his house. At the end of the day Alberto would begin the lengthy process of separating and counting all the coins from

BROKEN TREATY

the day's profits of all four tortillerias. Stephen told me he received a small commission for helping count all the coins every now and then and this collection was his savings. I shared his grin.

"We'll take it to my bank to see what it is worth to convert it into dollars if you like," I offered. I could see the accounting process in his head as he considered my proposal. I didn't realize it at the time but I was slipping back into the role of fatherhood, now letting a softer, inner intuition be my guide.

I badly wanted to talk to my dad. I knew from the brief conversation I had been allowed with him that they might still be worried, unaware that I had been released with Stephen in Brownsville. But there was no way to call on this smaller, United Airlines flight.

A flight attendant appeared next to me out of nowhere.

"You two look like you've had a pretty rough day," she said. "Can I get you something to drink?"

I couldn't keep it in. I had to share my elation with someone.

"This is my son. He's been missing for almost a year and a half. I rescued him out of Mexico just hours ago. We're headed back home to California."

The woman crossed her hands over her heart and sat down in the seat across the aisle. She studied us both for a moment and I saw the tears well up in her blue eyes. I wasn't anticipating such an emotional response. This was one of the first strangers I'd had contact with today that offered no complications.

"We're okay. We're fine," I assured her. I shared some of the details, being careful about what I said in the event Stephen could still understand some English. She excused herself and went for our beverages, returning after. "Congratulations. The beverages are on us," she said.

The orange juice was the first healthy thing I'd had in three days. It had an effect that was as calming as a stiff drink. Stephen was enjoying his Coca Cola and peanuts and over the next 20 minutes the entire crew of attendents came by to look us over and congratulate us on being back in the United States.

We both looked ridden hard and put away wet. My green, button-down long sleeve shirt had a powerful ripeness to it by now and I'd lost fistfuls of hair to Stephen in the drama of the struggle. Stephen wore the gray B.U.M. t-shirt I'd had him change into during the escape, but the dark green school-uniform slacks he still wore were somewhat tattered. This surprised me as Silvia typically bought by label, not value. The remaining shoe from the struggle looked like something found in a second-hand store that would never get beyond the cash register. On top of it all were the dark circles below Stephen's eyes. It concerned me and I wondered if he was malnourished.

It didn't make sense. From first-hand experience, I knew the routines and eating habits in the household. Food was always plentiful. He seemed underweight and his face somewhat gaunt. A visit to his pediatrician would be one of my first priorities if no one stopped us in Houston.

I was dying to know why he didn't get on the bus that first day when we were waiting. I did a little probing.

"Stephen, I was actually planning to bring you home yesterday, but you didn't get on the bus with all the other kids. Did you go to school at all yesterday?"

BROKEN TREATY

Stephen finished his glass of chilled coke and very nonchalantly replied: "Mom got up too late and didn't wake me up for school so I stayed home," Stephen said.

That so many variables had to align for the rescue to succeed was now beginning to sink in. A different day would have brought different circumstances: if a Mexican cop had stumbled on any leg of the rescue, if another bystander had tried to interfere, or if Stephen had had a change of heart and called out to the soldiers on the field, the outcome could have been disastrous.

As we talked I could feel the time and distance that had kept us apart beginning to evaporate. The knot in my stomach for the last 16 months was gone. Stephen told me about the two little white poodles at the house in Xalapa and about his bike that had five speeds. He told me that he didn't ride it much because his mother wouldn't let him take it into the street alone.

"I think that we should look into a new bike because you've grown so much." I said.

"Son, do you remember the model submarine we were working on when you left?" He paused for a moment, his eyes widening as he sat up in his seat. He clearly remembered.

"You didn't finish it did you?"

"Of course not, it's exactly the way you left it – so we could finish it together. We were getting ready to set the missiles into their bay hatches when you went to Mexico." His eyes lit up and I could see him trying to recall the submarine.

I had a precise memory on the project, passing by it every morning, careful not to disturb the model and its parts, envisioning the day we could finish it together. The subtle throttle-back of the engines indicated the plane's preparation to descend. I began to wonder what would happen when we emerged from the gate. Somehow, I would need to get word out if we were detained again. I scribbled some information on the back of my business card and walked back to where our kind flight attendant was stowing gear for landing. "I have a terrific favor to ask of you," I ventured.

I interpreted her smile as willingness to help.

"We ran into some awkwardness resulting from Mexico City's displeasure at the rescue back in Brownsville," I explained. "The D.A. there wanted us held but the FBI released us. I'm worried that, through some foul-up, we might get detained again leaving the plane in Houston. If that should happen, would you be willing to call these people and explain?"

She looked at me, smiled and said, "Yes, I'd be happy to help out."

I handed her the card. "Tom is my Dad, and this number is for Melanie Headrick, the D.A. investigator back in California. She helped us get out of Brownsville."

There was still a sense of urgency in my face revealing the seriousness of my request. "You and your son have had an interesting day, haven't you," she said.

I could only smile back and nod, appreciating her understatement. I returned to my seat feeling a little more confident, knowing that the right people would be informed and taking action if Stephen and I were detained again.

I waited for the other passengers to disembark, thinking it might add a little confusion to anyone looking for us. Besides, if Stephen were taken again, every lingering moment might be the last with him.

At the cabin exit we passed the flight attendant who had become my lifeline.

"I spoke to a friend at the gate and she says that nothing unusual is going on," she reassured.

I wondered if Mexico's allegations might have been stalled for the time being. The flight attendant's disclosure offered a level of confidence that Stephen and I might make it home, perhaps even tonight. I never learned her name, but I would never forget her relieved look as she shared what she knew.

We emerged from the arrival gate to find the Houston terminal as busy as a shopping mall on Christmas Eve. There was absolutely no interest in us. Folks were completely consumed in their own intents and pursuits. No one even noticed Stephen's tattered green slacks and lack of shoes.

Big problems were now replaced by little ones that I welcomed. I started making decisions. We would find our parting gate for the flight to San Francisco, then look for shoes in some of the shops, and make phone calls. I put phone calls as last priority with the understanding that there would be an Airfone in the seatback of the next flight.

We walked through the huge concourse both staring like hillbillies in a big city for the first time. We carried all of our gear, three bags in all. I was impressed with Stephen's stamina, lugging around his amassed fortune in coins while only wearing socks. Not once did he complain. Once we found our gate we went on the hunt for shoes. I still held out hope that now in Houston, we might at least find a souvenir shop that offered children's cowboy boots.

BROKEN TREATY

Stephen's small hand clutched mine as we wandered the concourse halls. We ventured through a half dozen or so shops without finding a single pair of boots or anything else that could pass as footwear. Meanwhile Stephen became interested in a magic set, which we bought along with his choice of gum.

Time cut our search short and I realized that the phone calls would have to wait until we were in the air. We returned to our departure gate just as boarding was announced. Taking our seats as the plane prepared for take-off, I eyed the Airfone that was embedded in the seatback in front of us. We found ourselves rolling down a runway for the third time on the last leg of the longest day of my life. The scheduled arrival in San Francisco was 9:35 p.m. local time. It was now 15 minutes in front of 6. We would be in San Francisco in about three hours. It occurred to me that time was now on my side. Still I knew I should be prudent with what lay ahead. I held my son's head to my shoulder and kissed him on his head.

Stephen started playing with the magic kit, and it wasn't long before I saw a coin disappear into a small black box. When I saw Stephen's eyes grow sleepy, I propped a pillow behind his head and fumbled for a credit card lifting the handset of the Airfone. My father Tom anticipated my call.

"Dad, we made it out of Brownsville. We've just left Houston with no problems and are on our way to San Francisco," I blurted out.

"We know," my Dad volleyed back. "You're on a United flight arriving at 9:35. Buckman's office has been calling all afternoon with updates on what was happening.

In a calmer and concerned voice, my dad said, "We know you've

BROKEN TREATY

been through hell, but we can imagine this has been toughest of all on Stephen. How is he doing?"

"He's doing relatively well, considering a near disaster after we landed in Brownsville. The Mexican consulate sent over an official intent on taking Stephen back to Mexico. He had a couple of hours to work on him before they let us go and he caused Stephen to panic. He wasn't happy about going any further at that point. I was so furious," I confided. My dad had a diplomatic style of diffusing tension by changing subjects.

"We've been on the phone all day with family and friends carefully following developments. You can expect a greeting committee at the gate when you arrive. Do you think it might be too overwhelming for Stephen, considering what he's just been through?" He asked. My response was immediate.

"Oh hell no Dad. It's time to celebrate his return. I want him to see that he's been missed by everyone.

"Well, then, expect a big welcome home," Dad assured.

"Dad, Stephen doesn't have any shoes. Could you ask someone to take a guess at his size and pick up a pair of tennis shoes? I'll explain why later," I told him.

"We already know. Your sister Mary is already on it. She'll be at the airport," he said.

"Dad, I need to tell you and Mom now, before the dust settles, that this couldn't have happened without your help, and I love you both so much. I'll never begin to be able to express in words how grateful I am. Thanks."

There was silence on his end before he responded. "Steve, aside from the terrible devastation of missing Stephen so much, we knew

BROKEN TREATY

what it was doing to you. Your mom and I have raised nine healthy children, and have, at last count, some 30 grandchildren. We saw your only child taken from you and couldn't stand by and watch your suffering. We're very elated and proud of you for bringing Stephen home and even happier to hear a spirit in your voice we feared we'd never hear again. Just get here safe with Stephen." By this time I had so many feelings swimming through my head, I was overwhelmed. I said goodbye to my dad.

I thought about my mom and dad and some of the short stories and tall laughs that were the character-building core for our family. I was bringing their grandson home now and perhaps they could get back to their well deserved golden years and start enjoying retirement, knowing that the family was intact with Stephen's return.

The engines slowly throttled back and we began our descent into San Francisco International Airport. I looked down at Stephen who had been fast asleep for the past two hours, his magic set scattered over his lap and the floor below. I gently nudged him. His eyes opened slowly and I could see his mind trying to answer questions his sleep had put aside. He realized his surroundings and began to adjust himself by sitting up. His eyes searched mine.

"¿Casi llegamos?" – "Are we almost there?" Stephen asked, in a surprisingly subtle manner.

"Yes, Son, we should be landing in about 20 minutes. If you look out the window, you can see right around where our home should be." I could only tell this because of the black outline of the bay where lights stopped at the waterline. Stephen watched in awe as the nightscape below passed quickly through the window frame during the descent. After a few minutes the seatbelt sign lit for landing. I used the moment to get Stephen's attention. I continued speaking to him in the only tongue he seemed to understand.

"Stephen, I know how tough this has been for you. You need to know that your mom is not a bad person she just did something she shouldn't have done. When she realizes what she needs to do to be with you, I'm sure she will be back in no time. What you need to know right now, is that there are a lot of people waiting for us to get off this plane, and many will smile and some will cry. Can you handle that?"

Stephen changed the subject. "I can't leave the plane to see everyone with no shoes, Dad!" he declared.

"I think we have it covered," I assured him. "Let's just see if there's a pair of tennis shoes waiting for you." He seemed satisfied with my answer. He grabbed his backpack full of coins and school books and held them close. Our flight arrived on time.

We were home.

BROKEN TREATY

BROKEN TREATY

Chapter 21

Back in California

The chaos back in Brownsville had left me wondering just how much time I'd be able to spend with Stephen before he might be taken away from me. The flight to Houston out of Brownsville had been less than an hour, but the flight to San Francisco had been three hours, giving Mexico City even more time to regroup and try to somehow convince any American authorities willing to listen to "grab Fenton and his son."

As the plane taxied to the terminal, I wanted to believe that we were home free. I felt that being so far from the border would offer some kind of protection based on geography alone. I hoped for a meeting exclusive of authorities or diplomats. As I helped Stephen collect his scattered magic set, I entertained an amusing thought of my mom's wrath that would be visited on any official that came between Stephen and his grandmother. Mom stands five-feet tall and possesses 90 pounds of ferocious fury when it came to defending her own family.

I prepared myself for anything as the crowded isle thinned out and I could now freely gather our few carry-on bags and move toward the cabin exit. Not certain about what the next moments had in store for us, I instinctively paused and knelt down at Stephen's side momentarily holding up the line. I took his heavy back-pack from him and offered, "I think I can carry you to a new pair of shoes. Would you like that, Son?"

"Si," he responded with a more dignified smile.

BROKEN TREATY

I hoisted Stephen once again to my hip as I had when we walked across the tarmac at El Lencero to Ed's plane. I shouldered the two heaviest bags on my left and the lightest in my right hand, jostling the load once again to counter Stephen's weight. We emerged from the cabin and followed the path through the gangway chute that funneled out to the arrival area.

The world slowed down slightly and I heard nothing as a panorama of faces now came into view. Glistening eyes turned toward us and, as they saw Stephen, there was a quiet buzz of excitement. I scanned the small sea of faces and sorted out family among friends, but I wouldn't stop to acknowledge anyone until I could look into the smiling face of my mother, Hilda.

I caught mom's comforting blue eyes, as her smile broadened. She had no way of knowing my new fears, but the moment our eyes met, there was a subliminal message that I no longer needed to look left or right to see if some authority was going to grab me or Stephen. I abandoned my paranoia; reading in her eyes the pride she felt at seeing her grandson home.

I moved toward my mother standing alongside my father. I could finally feel a more permanent sense of the rescue. No one was here to take Stephen from me. Two of my sisters held up a colorful 10-foot banner that had been unfurled with the words: "Welcome Home Stephen!"

No one spoke as the small crowd of family and friends encircled me and Stephen. I stopped, dropped the bags to the ground and gently lowered Stephen off my hip. Stephen moved toward his grandparents gaining comfort from their welcoming faces while understanding that his return had been greatly anticipated. Stephen

BROKEN TREATY

walked to my mom's open arms.

"We've all missed you so much, Stevie," she said softly as the two embraced. My father, typically not at a loss for words, watched with nearly paralyzing disbelief that his grandson had made it home. He grinned down at Stephen. Light, animated chatter began to rise from inspired voices as the small crowd now began to individually greet and welcome Stephen home. Mary stepped toward him. Even before he could reach out to hug her, Mary held out a Nike shoebox and lifted the top as she dropped to her knees in front of him.

"We understand that you had a footwear malfunction, so we picked up a pair of new Nikes for you. I hope they're close to your size," Mary said. She hadn't been told that Stephen no longer spoke English but it didn't matter much. Stephen didn't seem to realize that no one could understand him, or it simply didn't matter. I recited translations to Stephen as those around him spoke, but I was muted by the swirl of excitement. The language barrier had been removed before it could become a factor. Tonight, love and action made speech unnecessary. Mary lifted the lid to the shoe box as Stephen reached in, pulling aside the paper tissue over the shoes. Red flashes beaconed from the soles as his hand grasped the first shoe.

Mary helped Stephen into the shoes and began the lacing process, while grinning family members gathered around still numb from Stephen's abrupt return from Mexico. He mustered all the patience he could while his cousin Kyle, only a year older than Stephen, hovered, battling patience, watching the laces pass through eyelets. Kyle hadn't understood the complexities of Stephen's absence but was terribly anxious to help welcome him home.

BROKEN TREATY

Kyle set a course and had already made several yards on Stephen as the two cousins broke in the new Nikes. My pride and elation soared as I watched Stephen and his cousin chasing each other.

I was jolted with panic as Stephen disappeared into the vastness of the airport concourse of a thousand people with unclear intentions. I kept my composure; my heart palpitating until Stephen emerged from the shadows chasing Kyle.

I had reckoned early on that there might be fallout from my unorthodox method of reunification, but the mess that we encountered in Brownsville was much more than I had expected. Stephen and I both believed his mother would not be far behind to initiate whatever damage control was necessary to arrange access to Stephen. At some point she would be responsible for rebuilding the bridges. My job was to offer some degree of normalcy to Stephen's future and get back into some old routines.

But now it was time to celebrate, and the terrific crowd gathering seemed to have a powerful reassuring effect on Stephen. The energy in the arrival area was as soothing as a balmy evening breeze; eager smiles and reassuring hugs underscored how much he had been missed. The people that he almost forgot had come to see him home and many more would be surfacing over the days to come.

I had asked my dad to bring my Toyota 4Runner to the airport. Stephen had helped me choose the car only a couple of months before he was taken. A caravan of ecstatic revelers headed south along the freeway toward my parent's home in Los Altos. The enthusiasm helped distract Stephen from the thoughts that he must have had about his Mom, the abrupt removal from his school and classmates and everything else he had come to know over the last

BROKEN TREATY

16 months. I was plenty angry with Silvia for what she had done and the resulting drama and perhaps trauma-to-come to our son, but I was not going to perpetuate the animosity through Stephen. Though he had assumed a noble attitude about agreeing to let us escape out of Xalapa, I knew that he loved his mother and all that I could offer at this time was my unwavering love and assurance that the madness was over.

At my parent's home, Stephen found much as it had been and seemed to gain security from familiarity. Walking into the house with him still seemed surreal. I wondered when my euphoria would subside. I wanted to celebrate but I couldn't seem to get beyond the feeling that it was all a dream. The home filled like a college pick-up party and half a dozen pizzas were ordered.

Early into the morning as relatives departed, I let Stephen settle into a large bed with his cousin Kyle. The boys laughed themselves to sleep watching late night cartoons.

With Stephen thus occupied, I joined the remaining family members downstairs. They had been trying to piece together the bits of information they had from Buckman's office after we were detained in Brownsville. I took calls from family members who hadn't been able to make it out on such short notice, but would be on their way.

I didn't go into detail but gave an overview of what had taken place. I hadn't wanted to spoil the spirit of the homecoming. At this moment, everything was exactly the way it was supposed to be. We stayed that evening at my parents. I sprawled out in a reclining chair next to the bed where the boys slept. I did not sleep well and easily awoke to the sound of a car circling into the cul-de-sac of the

BROKEN TREATY

quiet suburban home at 3:30 in the morning.

Chapter 22

Sisterhood of the pantalones

In the morning, Stephen woke with a grin, perhaps a gentle shift from a pleasant dream or maybe restful recovery from the exhausting struggle. I lay next to Stephen and cradled him as he became reacquainted with his old surroundings. Kyle came to and brought the TV back to life, surfing the channel offerings with the remote. An old Beavus and Butthead cartoon launched the boys into hysterics and gave me a chance to study his English comprehension. I saw that it was a combination of Kyle's reaction and the visuals of the animation cuing his laughter. Stephen and I had only spoken in Spanish, but with no other option he began to look to me for translation if he took any interest in dialogue around him.

The smell of cooking bacon and scrambled eggs from my mom's kitchen wafted up to greet me at the stairwell when Buckman called. My mom cut her hug short, giving me a look that made it clear she expected me to give her all the details. I had assumed Buckman made it out of Texas, but I would never forget the panic in his eyes as I was led away by the jumbo size customs officer in Brownsville.

"How is Stephen doing?" he asked.

"Actually Pat, considering what happened, I'm surprised he's as relaxed as he is. I think that we're both still in shock. What happened to you in Brownsville?"

"I have to say that this rescue was a little too close for me. This might be my last one," he prefaced, before taking a breath to continue.

BROKEN TREATY

My grip tightened around the phone.

"No one was interested in me luckily, but Ed's plane was impounded while they held you. I started making calls as soon as I landed in Houston. Headrick's office was already on this by the time we contacted them. Apparently the state attorney's office and Senator Feinstein's office jumped all over the Justice Department to get you released while Mexico City literally made a federal case to get your son sent back to Mexico. They insisted that you assaulted a school bus with automatic weapons fire, that we hijacked the Cherokee at gunpoint, presented false docs and that your son had a Mexican birth certificate. I've never seen this kind of reaction from another country after a rescue, let alone Mexico.

"After the last car switch, Mike drove on to catch a flight out of Veracruz a few hours after we took off in the Cherokee. He said police were crawling all over the airport looking for you and Stephen. Mexico City persuaded officials here to have U.S. Immigration and Customs looking for you and your son in every U.S. port of entry.

"Your father in-law must have a lot more influence than you mentioned. Mexico is furious and the State Department is officially condemning your actions," Buckman said.

I thought about Elizabeth Wadium, my State Department caseworker who had rerouted me to deal directly with the Mexican Central Authority. Essentially, I had become my own caseworker. Wouldn't she be discreetly high-fiving her co-workers at the news of the rescue?

"Look Steve, your wife's family is looking at Stephen as a trophy. My guess is that they're going to try to light a fire under any authority or bribable official to reverse this, which is highly unlikely. When that road leads to a dead end, they may try to take him. You're going to have to be careful from now on," he said.

His analysis only validated my concern of a long-term threat from across the border. I didn't bother asking about his sources based on his past reluctance to comment. I accepted what he felt I needed to know, not worrying about things that didn't matter.

Buckman and I agreed to share any information that came our way; however, I did get the feeling that he'd prefer to limit any unnecessary contact for now. Besides, he had performed on our contract.

It was time to call Melanie Headrick. After Buckman's summary I was anxious about how the D.A.'s office would treat the rescue. Melanie had been the same investigator for the other father, Dave, who had rescued his son off the island in the West Indies only months earlier. Melanie called me when she had first learned about that rescue and was grateful for the recovery but could not endorse the means.

After a personal declaration of her own exhilaration about Stephen's return, she gave her account of the most critical point in the dialogue with the FBI in Brownsville.

"Steve…I was at lunch with some of the other investigators when the call from your dad came through. It took an hour to get through to Hutchins, the FBI special agent holding you. He indicated that they were getting ready to hand Stephen over to the Mexican Consulate official and hold you on federal kidnapping charges. Mexico City had been adamant that all of your documents were forgeries, along with assault with weapons and aircraft theft. They weren't going to even tell you when they'd taken Stephen.

BROKEN TREATY

"That was when I stopped Hutchins and gave him a 60-second download of the brutal realities of your case. I asked him if he owned a home, because he would most likely lose it after the lawsuits that would be headed his way if Stephen were sent back to Mexico without verifying your California custody orders. I told him it was going to be a complete travesty of justice if Stephen was taken back. From the silence I could tell he'd only heard the Mexican side of the situation. He said that he would look into it. Apparently, the FBI rushed one of their agents to the Court Records office here in town, to verify your orders. I was told to call back but never got through again. The FBI had been so swamped by so many agencies and officials calling on your behalf, we only found out you and Stephen had been released after you got on the plane for Houston," Melanie said.

She clearly went above and beyond the call of duty. I would have expected a much less compassionate demeanor in view of her constant exposure to squabbling parents. But she cared so much that I wondered how she made it this long as I recalled the countless faces of missing children from case files that decorated her cubicle.

"Can you imagine if this happened over the weekend with every agency and courthouse closed?" she added.

I remembered how she had entrusted me with her private phone number early on, so she could be reached at any time of any day. I was at a loss, besieged by her vivid description of what I had only speculated on before. It was becoming clear that the urgency in Texas wasn't purely panic on my part. I had half thought that maybe the FBI was toying with me to see if I might give them a reason to hold me, but Buckman and Melanie confirmed my concern.

BROKEN TREATY

"You might be interested to know, Steve, that I had started getting frequent calls from higher-ups at the State Department asking what you were up to and if I knew where you were each time they called. This was unusual – as if they had somehow known you would be trying this on your own. I don't know what made them suspicious," she added.

Melanie eagerly opened her schedule for me to bring Stephen by the next afternoon. This would be the greatest demonstration of gratitude considering the recovery rate for cross border abductions had "insufficient data." She had only met a handful of recovered children in her sixth year as a lead child abduction investigator for the D.A.'s office.

Resuming my role as a dad, I had to remind myself that I was Stephen's only parental source for love and affection, although the compassion demonstrated by my family was a great help. My sisters doted on him almost more than on their own.

One of the biggest issues I hadn't considered was that Stephen had no clothing except for the T-shirt, sweatshirt and pants I'd taken with me, and they had been only a guess at his size. My sisters Mary and Connie met us at the airport, but my youngest sister, Karen, had been in Washington, D.C., on business and caught the next flight back to California as soon as she heard the news about my return with Stephen. The three sisters, aware that I was nearly penniless from the costs of the rescue, herded Stephen and me into a mini-van for a shopping spree.

"What kind of new clothes do you need the most, Stephen?" Karen asked.

BROKEN TREATY

After a quick moment reflecting on my translation, Stephen excitedly cried out: "pantalones"—"pants."

The sisters swarmed into the boy's clothing section at a department store, guiding Stephen to the dressing room, each sister with an armload of clothes. The three girls made such a commotion that a man in a nearby stall complained to the clerk about the privacy invasion, though my sisters paid the man no mind.

We returned from the shopping adventure with a new wardrobe for Stephen. My older brother, Mike, had arrived from Fresno bringing a gift for Stephen, introducing him to a new baseball card collection.

While I got Stephen set up to shower himself for the first time before putting on his new clothes, I made an appointment with his pediatrician. Aside from the need for a complete physical, the dark areas under his eyes and low weight had me concerned. I also arranged for a conference with the principal at his old school. There were less than seven weeks of class left for the school year. The fact that he no longer spoke English would be an issue that I would wait to deal with in person, summoning all the persuasiveness I could muster. The best thing I believed for Stephen now was to get him as occupied as possible with constant manageable challenges, with reassurance that he is loved dearly and is safe.

On the morning of the second day of his homecoming, we had two very important visits planned. We stopped in to see the staff at the Vanished Children's Alliance. Georgia Hilgeman the founder, along with Gail Wood, my caseworker, prepared a staff party for Stephen, with cake, balloons, cards and a photographer. The organization offers help on a national level, all through private contributions.

BROKEN TREATY

It was evident that they rarely got to personally welcome a child home, even more seldom a victim of international abduction. The excitement was nearly pandemic.

Our next stop was Melanie Headrick's office, where we were asked to wait outside in the lawn area for her to greet us. She had warned me that it would be best not to let the walls that had become a collage of the faces of missing children be a reminder of Stephen's ordeal. She greeted Stephen with a subtle glow, trying to make light conversation, but the language barrier was limiting. With gentle patience, she let me casually translate her comments and his replies. I hadn't gone into detail with Stephen on her involvement, but he understood, as he had at the celebration we'd just attended, that Melanie had been only interested in his return. When Melanie said goodbye, I thought about the pile of missing faces that waited back in her office. "If any of them has a chance, it will be with Melanie," I thought to myself making our way through the parking lot.

Later in the day I received a call from Bill Hilton, the attorney. I was apprehensive about taking his call. In my mind, he was no longer needed, seeing that Stephen had been returned to California. I assumed that the Hague Convention Treaty petition would be dismissed.

"Not that simple," Hilton said.

"What are you saying, Bill?" I probed.

"What you have to consider is that nothing could stop your wife from filing her own Hague petition with the courts in Mexico. What I highly recommend that you ask the State Department to consider the case resolved to finalize it. That would prohibit her from ever filing a new petition, keeping you in court indefinitely," he said.

BROKEN TREATY

I half expected I'd never hear from Bill again, or if I did, assumed he would have disapproved of my method. But I couldn't see any flaws in his reasoning.

"I'm not too sure that the State Department cares much about my position on anything right about now, Bill. I don't think they're going to be much help," I replied.

"You let me handle that. I just need you to confirm that you want to see the case resolved through The Hague Court, eliminating the chances for an appeal," he said.

Bill had been more cost effective than any other legal pursuit to date. I even recalled that funds were still available from the initial retainer. I saw his argument and asked him to proceed. I only worried that the State Department might see this as an opportunity to express their displeasure by rejecting a Hague resolution in retaliation. At the very least, I felt that keeping Bill involved might help divert any menace headed my way. The conversation concluded with an understanding – courteous, but formal. If he'd allowed himself any joy at Stephen's return, he kept a good poker face.

A call that I couldn't put off any longer was the National Center for Missing and Exploited Children to share the news of Stephen's rescue. The thrill in the woman's voice who took my information to close Stephen's file was ecstatic. She understood what I'd been up against trying to get a child out of Mexico. She commented on how rare recoveries were in international cases and privately supported my resourcefulness, but could not officially endorse my means.

I felt compelled to contact the State Department and my caseworker, but decided not to push it. Equally, no good could come out of following up with the Mexican Central Authority in

BROKEN TREATY

Mexico City. They were most likely aware of what happened in Xalapa before we even landed in Brownsville, though I couldn't help but imagine Laura Duclaud trying to hold back a smile when she heard the news. My personal appearance and plea with her at the Mexican Central Authority headquarters seemed to have the greatest impact on her. I felt bad about the politics that prevented me from making contact.

BROKEN TREATY

BROKEN TREATY

CHAPTER 23

BACK TO SCHOOL

I was torn between living under the radar by putting Stephen in a new school, or resuming his life as he had known it. By keeping him in the same school I could count on support from my family nearby to get him to and from school when I could not. He would have to be escorted to the classroom and picked up every day as soon as the bell rang. Paranoia and extreme vigilance produce the same outcome in the long run.

I had contacted the principal about the situation when he was taken, explaining he might be absent for an extended period, but I had always assured her and Stephen's teacher at the time that he would be returning. I surmised that no one at the school actually had expected to see him again. Now that he was home, I made an appointment to discuss Stephen's situation and my concerns about his safety. I pleaded to have him re-registered with so few weeks left in the school year.

"We are eager to have him back, but you should consider that there are only about six weeks of classes left and that means no time to assess him. Have you thought about getting him acclimated to life at home before jumping back into classes," she said.

She wasted no time sugar coating the issue, but I let her finish.

"You've explained that he lost his English. That could prove difficult for his teacher as well as progress for the other students. Maybe it would be better to start him in the fall?" she suggested.

Stephen had been kept back to repeat kindergarten once already.

BROKEN TREATY

I wasn't going to let the harm to his education continue. I knew that by law, the school had to accept Stephen back into class. I felt confident that he'd pick up English fast and the total immersion method was the most effective path.

"You'll see that his English will come back in no time. Besides could you think of a better way to get back into his routine than picking up with his old friends?" I asked, hoping she would see the sense of my argument. She reluctantly agreed.

I filled out the registration forms in her office before leaving. He would start school on Monday.

The next morning Stephen and I traveled to his pediatrician, Dr. Foster, for his exam. I had a chance to explain briefly in private to Dr. Foster about the rescue and my concerns about not only his health, but his psychological state as well. He had been my pediatrician and it was reassuring to have his expertise in Stephen's corner.

"The dark circles look more like some kind of allergy, perhaps from animals or a diet that doesn't agree with him," the doctor explained.

"Does he seem underweight?" I asked.

"He could use some fat on him. If he's okay with milk, let him drink all he wants. Other than that he looks healthy, and he is still current on immunizations," he indicated.

Milk wasn't an option with meals in Mexico because reliable refrigeration and the short shelf life prohibited it. Coca Cola had cornered the market.

"One thing that you might want to consider at his age is soccer. The game helps develop motor skills and gets some of the wiggles out for a good sleep at night. Of all the sports I've coached, soccer seems to hold the best interest for kids at any level. They don't need to know the rules, they just run and have fun!" he offered.

Before leaving the exam room with Stephen, I ventured to ask what he thought about Stephen's psyche.

"Children are more resilient than adults give them credit for. It's part of their survival mechanism to push bad experiences out of the way. Regardless, he will miss his mother. You need to watch for unusual periods of silence or despondent behavior that sometimes indicate depression. Keep him active and let him play with his friends," he added.

Stephen said little during the exam, but asked upon leaving Dr. Foster's office where we might buy baseball cards to add to the collection that my brother had given him. We went to a card and baseball shop I remembered from years back. He was drawn to the more rare cards inside the glass display. He made a careful selection with a budget guideline I offered. On the way out he asked if we might be able to go to my bank to get an appraisal on the coins he still had in his backpack from Mexico.

I'd been rapidly exhausting the cash reserves from the rescue – all that I had to my name. Still, the thought of raising a child was euphoric no matter the cost. Considering where my cash had gone for the last year and a half, I needed to get back to work.

There was a big homecoming celebration organized for his first weekend back, bringing together the most familiar faces from his life before being taken. The weekend weather turned out to be brilliant, perfect for an outdoor barbeque. He had lost the gaunt look and circles under his eyes. As his interaction with others intensified, he became more aware of his language limitations, but spoke to everyone in Spanish as if it were only a different style of speech. His relatives countered by figuring he'd ask me for a translation if the need arose. Stephen was deluged with "welcome home" gifts.

The intensity of my family's support extended beyond the miracle of his return. They understood the emotional impact of the rescue and were sensitive to his mom's absence. No one spoke ill of her around him and promoted positive feelings when he mentioned her, but that was rare. The fact that he preferred not to talk about his mother or life in Xalapa early on was understandable, though I encouraged anything he'd care to share when it suited him. I was concerned that he might be ashamed of his mother's behavior. I also wondered when we might hear something from her.

I had one more full week of leave from work to help Stephen become accustomed to being home and to going to school. I let go of his hand as Stephen's old friends from kindergarten ran toward him. They asked every awkward question a curious boy could dream up. They demanded to know why he'd been away for so long. I figured that the cross examination would be short lived and the jury would recess before any of the kids gave it a second thought—that is if any of them could understand a response from him.

His time in school allowed me to follow up with anyone that still had not heard the news and to get a reading on anything I should be concerned about. I was aware of the potential for emotional trauma to victims of abduction and contacted a child therapist who specialized in working with recovered children. I gave her a synopsis of the rescue over the phone and she suggested I bring Stephen in for an evaluation one day after school, which we scheduled.

BROKEN TREATY

The next day I received a phone call from the Mexican Central Authority. It was the voice of a lower ranking staff member that I had spoken with only a couple of times back when I was in daily contact with that office. He wasted no time in English.

"Mr. Fenton, we understand that you have recovered your son back to the United States and that you no longer have a case with this office. There are some documents that need your attention and we want to confirm that the phone number we have for you will serve for a fax. Can you give me that phone number Mr. Fenton?" The man asked.

"Yes, it is the same number as before, where you forwarded all the other documents," I responded. I hadn't recalled such a formal tone from anyone at the MCA office before.

"Thank you, Mr. Fenton, the documents will be faxed to you in the next few minutes. Please read them over carefully," the voice instructed before hanging up.

As the fax machine began scrolling out pages of text with signatures and official seals, I realized I was being legally summoned. Legalese in any language isn't my long suit but I could pick out enough to understand the implications. I was being ordered to appear in Mexico City at a federal court hearing June 8th at 10:30 A.M. to answer federal kidnapping charges.

I called Bill Hilton to tell him of the development.

"I would advise you that if you attend the hearing you will not likely leave the court the same way you went in. The Mexicans must realize that you won't show up, but it's most likely part of a legal process. What they are up to – I can't say. But you must have really upset them. I work with the MCA on a regular basis and I've never seen this kind of interest even after a self-sanctioned recovery like yours. The phony flight plan along with the weapons claim probably got the Mexican attorney general's attention," he said.

"Christ almighty, Bill, I was doing the job they were supposed to do. They ought to be grateful that I won't be taking up their time anymore!" I burst out.

"They are offended and probably feel the need to take a proactive posture. This will probably all blow away with time. Stay put. Don't go to Mexico and don't talk to any Mexican officials," he concluded.

I never considered for a moment appearing in court in Mexico City but it instilled confidence having Hilton in agreement. However, the unprecedented posture by Mexico City only added to my worries. I would consider every day that I readied Stephen for school, got him home, read to him in bed and kissed him good night to be one more day toward the day that he would be too old to be taken again.

Social skills were a natural gift for Stephen. He has an uncanny gift at befriending people. Kids were drawn to him and he never had an enemy that I knew of. Even with the language barrier, I was certain that he would re-establish old friendships and start new ones at the first recess of his first class. By the second day, he was being heartily greeted by nearly every schoolmate within earshot, coming and going. He always held my hand to and from the door and was never shy to say, "I love you."

One morning toward the end of the week, the principal approached me.

"We have had a staff meeting regarding security issues with Stephen. We won't release him to anyone who is not signed off to take him from class. Stephen is quite a likeable young man and he has made so many friends so quickly," she prefaced.

I had an uneasy feeling about what was coming.

"But, his teacher is concerned that the language is an issue and that he won't be able to catch up with the class fast enough to move on to second grade. In reality, Mr. Fenton, we are finding that he can't understand the class material and he has no English reading skills at all," she explained.

If I stalled in my response she might assume that I could be convinced.

"Forgive me for disagreeing, I don't think we should give up just yet. He has made terrific strides at home and he is learning more English every day. He doesn't need to have me translate as much in just the short time he's been home," I told her.

I hoped that she wouldn't have the energy to dispute me if she saw how opposed I was to her suggestion.

"Stephen is going to pick up English faster than anyone can imagine. Aside from going over the school work he just started bringing home, we're reading every night for at least an hour before bedtime. He's repeated kindergarten once already. I think it will be a bad move to send him back into first grade again. You will see improvement by next week. I promise," I pleaded.

"Pour it on at home. Maybe he can gain on it. Just keep in mind that he will probably have to attend summer school to help get him ready for second grade in the fall. That might get him there," she added.

I left feeling that the challenge to Stephen's ability to regain his English skills was relatively minor compared to the one I had just overcome with his principal.

We had the appointment with the child abduction therapist the same afternoon. I came in for the appointment early and let her take Stephen for an evaluation while I filled out paper work that provided a brief written account. I figured I would be present, but she wanted to see Stephen alone. Fair enough, but unless she was bilingual, there would be a problem. She ended the session after 20 minutes, explaining that the language barrier created an issue with her ability to talk with him about his time in Mexico.

The woman was uncommonly sympathetic, refusing to let me pay for her time. She advised bringing him back when his English returned, and cautioned about the warning signs as Dr. Foster had mentioned regarding withdrawal, silence and depression.

When I had a free moment one morning, I made a private and anxious phone call to my contact in Xalapa. I had broken off contact before the rescue to avoid implicating him, aware he could face retaliation from Alberto. In his first few words I understood that my call might have just complicated his life and career.

"La linea esta bloqueada," — "The line is tapped," the subdued voice said.

He'd somehow become a suspect. Although he knew nothing about the rescue. I ignored his comment.

"I just wanted to let you know that I finally got my son home and that he is very safe and healthy," I said. I ended our call not even able to thank him; realizing that we would probably never speak again. I called my attorney in Xalapa, Sr. Zurutuza, figuring that he at least owed me information from the balance of my retainer to him.

"Te aviso que la linea esta bloqueada,"—"I must warn you that this line is tapped," Sr. Zurutuza said. "The line of our mutual friend is tapped as well; so, you will not want to make contact with that person either."

If Zurutuza was going to talk freely, it would not be over the phone.

By his second week home, the drama of the rescue seemed to be receding. We both accepted our simpler, more routine challenges. I had no shortage of things to worry about, but I was grateful to be able to meet any issues head-on. The trauma Stephen had been through, as well adjusted as he might appear, would surface sooner or later. I privately hoped it would manifest early on while I could anticipate it rather than remain suppressed and show up later.

With support from my parents helping with afternoon care for Stephen, I prepared to get back to work.

BROKEN TREATY

Steve enrolled Stephen in a soccer league and the boy was good at it.

Chapter 24

Courts and Sports

Spring in our area of California is hard to beat. Skies are often a brilliant blue and the air still. This spring especially, I wanted to be home to share it with my son. Friends from work had given Stephen a new bike as a homecoming gift. His life in Mexico didn't permit him to ride the new five-speed bike he'd been given in Xalapa. I had the honor of teaching my son to ride twice. We rode nearly every day after I got home, exploring new streets and bike paths around our peaceful neighborhood in the late afternoons and early evenings.

After dinner, we spent time finishing off the model submarine that waited undisturbed. He insisted on me handling the more intricate portions of the assembly, but my hands didn't move fast enough to keep up with his enthusiasm – often observing so intently his head blocked my view.

Each night questions about his schoolwork and assignments became more specific. He began trying to sound out vowels and consonants in Spanish before I would repeat the English pronunciation, his eyes studying my lips to mimic them. Far from feeling bitter about his loss of English, I embraced his Spanish, worrying more about him losing his new gift than others worried about him re-mastering English. The fact that he had set aside one language to grasp a new one in the time he was gone suggested that a fast reversal loomed. For the time being, we spoke in Spanish with the exception of reading at bedtime. This had been our private time since he was a toddler. His mind captured images in books long before any language could have had any meaning. Although highly active, books never failed to draw his wonderment, asking to have his favorites read over and over. He seemed to enjoy familiar children's books again and again.

I began to notice that each night he was recognizing more dialogue from his old favorites. With increasing frequency he began slowly repeating the words to himself, comparing how they sounded against mine. Each night he grew more confident and applied a little more volume to each word. By the end of his second week back in school he was fluent again in English. His teacher and principal were dumbfounded. Even I hadn't been prepared for such an astonishing recovery. An adorable Spanish accent lingered for another two weeks before disappearing entirely. Although I continued to speak to him in Spanish, he had little use for it.

Sleepover invitations and birthday parties began to fill Stephen's social calendar. Baseball season for his age group was nearly over, but we did get signed up for soccer to begin in the fall. Even though he had good motor skills, the concept of belonging to a group as a uniformed team member had little appeal for him. The season was four months out—plenty of time to forget and let his apprehension go for now. I had my old first baseman's mitt and I let him throw to me one evening after biking. He surprised himself discovering his own throwing arm. We had a new mitt for him by the next evening and from then on threw together nearly every night after biking. My intention had been to occupy our lives with enough activity that Stephen wouldn't have time to reflect on his mother's judgment.

Still, not a day went by that I didn't worry how his mother's

BROKEN TREATY

absence from his life might impact his self-esteem. My private sentiments about her actions, then and even now, fluctuate from anger to pity. I scolded myself for letting her occupy space in my head, though my concern was never about her, but rather the damage from her decisions.

As Mother's Day came around I suggested that Stephen pick out a card and write her a letter. We included a recent photo and sent the letter to my sister in Washington to be forwarded with a Seattle postmark, to create confusion on our location. Just over a month after the rescue, I sensed – judging by her silence and knowing her pride – she had no immediate plans to return. The fact that I had assured Stephen that she would return almost immediately to California to handle her issues and somehow continue in his life, haunted me. I wanted to let it go, to convince myself that I had to step back. The situation was beyond my control.

Toward the end of May my dad called to tell me that I had been served through an attorney for Silvia with a summons to appear in local family court. The motion demanded that Stephen be immediately returned to Mexico. Silvia was claiming that the custody papers I had served on her in Mexico were not valid. She claimed she never received the paperwork.

The news triggered the same anxiety I'd endured while he was missing. My stomach began to knot up again. The documents instructed me to bring Stephen to the hearing. I was in disbelief. The glow and livelihood I'd recovered since Stephen's return was gone. I didn't understand how this could be allowed to happen. I'd believed litigation, courtrooms and attorneys were all behind me. I had only begun to start managing small incremental payments to my parents and older brother Tommy for their help that would take years to settle. Bill Hilton handled only International Child Abduction cases. There was too much at stake to bungle this on my own. I'd have to find a sharp specialist and then somehow come up with a retainer.

After interviewing attorneys over the next couple of days, I met with Brad Baugh. His reputation was legendary and I found him to be direct and honest. He made no cocky promises. Mr. Baugh sat up when Buckman's name was mentioned.

"Pat Buckman, the private investigator?" He queried. "Buckman is famous for what he does and he's the best. How the hell did you get his help?"

Based on Baugh's reaction to Buckman's name, I wondered if I had known everything there was to know about Pat.

"Forget about bringing your son to court, I'm not going to let that happen. Also, if what you are telling me is true about the felony kidnapping charges, she'll be arrested if she shows up in court," he explained.

Baugh was intrigued and seemed to take a more personal interest in the case, but it didn't get me a break on his retainer. I did, however, get the same confident feeling I got with Buckman – no arrogance or pointless rhetoric, and no guarantees. He gave me a couple of days to arrange the retainer. My father had anticipated my need before I even had to approach him, asking whom to make the check out to.

The hearing took place at 1:30 p.m. July 11. During the hearing, Stephen was with my father, who had been instructed to stand by his phone if developments warranted. Pat Buckman was on phone standby as well, on Baugh's request. While waiting outside the courtroom, Bill Hilton approached me. I figured he was there at court for another case.

"Another Hague case Bill?" I asked

"No, I'm representing your wife at this hearing. Didn't you know?" he replied.

The silence on my part was deafening. Bill saw that he'd gone too far with his opening joke and smiled as he explained the real reason he was here.

"The law prohibits me from representing your wife since I am already representing you," Bill said. "Actually I'm here representing you. Brad asked me to comment to the judge on the technical aspects of your court documents for custody abroad," he explained.

Only moments before Bill found me, I was stunned to see Silvia's younger sister, who had come all the way from Xalapa, most likely to take Stephen back if things went in their favor.

"Bill, don't you think that the judge is going to dismiss the entire motion since she can't even show up? Is there really any chance that the judge would send Stephen back to Mexico after all that's happened?" I reasoned.

Bill's answer was simple: "There is no way of knowing what a judge will do in any case."

With two of the most prominent attorney's in the county – each in their respective specialities – I couldn't believe the motion had a chance. Thank God it was denied. Hilton defended my due process of service in Xalapa citing "guard gate service" – considered proper legal service to anyone who came to the large steel gated entry to the home in Xalapa. Baugh argued to the judge that no further custody motion should be allowed following the lawful appeal timeframe, stipulating that no case could be heard unless Silvia appeared in court.

I didn't consider the judgment any kind of victory. I had only countered a frivolous legal motion. Silvia had found a pro-bono lawyer though, while claiming in a declaration that racial prejudice against Latinos prevented her from appearing in court on her own behalf. Regardless of her approach, I began to wonder if I would ever be done with litigation and the devastating financial implications. Bill Hilton mentioned before leaving court that the State Department ignored his requests to declare my case resolved, but that there was still some balance left on my original retainer with him. I didn't completely consider our business finalized so did not ask for the refund. Brad Baugh insisted that I now file a motion for divorce to finish the marriage through his office. Since Silvia would not likely appear in court, the matter would be "divorce by default" ending automatically six months after filing. Though divorce documents are expensive papers to push through any court, my additional legal fees were another blow, equaling the original retainer amount. I had to make a payment arrangement with Baugh to settle over time.

Instead of dwelling on defeating the court motion, I found escape in the evenings with Stephen on empty baseball diamonds, freed up now that Little League season had ended. The snap of a hardball into soft leather is good for the soul and doesn't cost anything.

The condition placed by the school on Stephen advancing to the second grade was that he complete a six-week summer session. I teased that the "extra innings at summer school would let him slide into second." The light homework load for summer school freed up time at night, and the lingering summer daylight freed up more time for play.

There was no direct attempt by Silvia to contact Stephen and I was privately losing interest in her future with our son if she had none. The only remote effort on her part was having the Mexican consulate in San Jose contact Brad Baugh to ask that I bring Stephen down to the consulate for a visit. Baugh recommended against it, reminding me that the consulate is technically on Mexican soil and that it could get complicated. I knew that Baugh had been in considerable dialogue with the consulate office because his monthly statement totaled over $400 in extra charges for his phone time with the Mexicans. I directed him not to take any more calls on my behalf from the consulate.

I felt that Silvia was at least consistent in her behavior – unwilling to be accountable and holding her own interests above her son's. I could not replace the sweet smells of his mother's soft embrace, but we hugged often and we never parted without saying: "I love you." Quality or not, my time was always his.

I kept the continuing drama from him, trying not to let him worry that he was anything but safe.

While I believed time was on my side, Mexico City used the last three months to pursue an unprecedented action that followed me to California.

BROKEN TREATY

Chapter 25

The rattle of machetes

Melanie Headrick's call came in on a late August afternoon, only six weeks after believing the last legal challenge was behind me.

"The district attorney has received a formal request to have you prosecuted for felony kidnapping along with weapons and other charges," she announced.

Numbness radiated through my body. I struggled for a response. "What should I do now, Melanie? What's going to happen? What about Stephen? Will I need another attorney?" I desperately asked. I had a hundred more questions.

"Look, Steve, there is no way of knowing what the D.A. is going to do. The only thing that we can be certain of is that the D.A. has to look at it and consider the request. Mexico seems to understand that no one is sending Stephen back to Mexico, but they appear to have it in for you."

"How can I get more information, Melanie?" I pleaded.

"The D.A. won't release any details. They are extremely tight lipped about this, but I will let you know as soon as I hear something," Melanie offered.

While an extradition treaty exists between Mexico and the U.S., the agreement only applies to respective nationals; a request for prosecution by authorities in the U.S. was the only option for Mexico City. The relative issue at hand was whether authorities in the U.S. would consider my actions a crime, regardless of how

BROKEN TREATY

virtuous my cause. The only thing certain was that I would not be consulted on any decision by any authority at any level.

Beyond the thought of securing an understanding with my sister Mary and the help of my parents to raise Stephen if I got sent away, Melanie's revelation prepared me for the worst. I accepted the fact that forces were still trying to separate Stephen and me. I never took one hug or goodnight kiss from Stephen for granted, but I didn't burden him. I would do the worrying for the both of us.

Soccer teams had been established early in August and I reminded Stephen about my request to give it two weeks before allowing him to quit. He was reluctant to put on his new soccer shoes for the first team practice.

I had seen a growing need for Stephen to hold my hand. In crowds he held my hand with the both of his. I believed it to be some kind residual trauma from the rescue. He was not eager to take the field, but knew a couple of the other boys from class and that helped him get into the first practice. He didn't let me get very far from sight, turning completely around to find me at times. When he saw that I wasn't going anywhere, he turned his attention on the ball and showed some surprising ball handling skills. I was so excited to see his surprising talent that I dashed to my truck to grab my camera. I had been away for only a few minutes and returned to find Stephen crying and one of the coaches trying to console him. Stephen had realized that I was absent and began to panic. I realized that this was a by-product from the drama of the rescue. Only after I promised not to disappear again would he return to the field. On the way home, he was enthusiastic about the practice.

"Dad, I think I really like soccer. I want to play on the team, but

BROKEN TREATY

you have to promise me that you will stay for the whole practice, and you can't leave," he announced.

The afternoon practices were late enough in the afternoons that I could meet this commitment with a little juggling at work.

"I didn't know that you could play like that Son! Did you play in Mexico?" I quizzed.

"Yes, we played every day at school, but it's called futbol not soccer."

Stephen's panic at soccer practice signaled it was time to seek some professional help. I found a child psychologist, and arranged a series of four weekly visits for him to evaluate Stephen. I hoped that early assessment would help identify and head off emotional issues that were bound to surface eventually. I had an initial 30-minute visit with one of the counselors to describe my concerns. I had a good feeling about the staff and was eager to get an evaluation and a recommendation based on their findings.

As soccer season got under way, school was not far behind and so was Stephen's eighth birthday – all within three weeks. My sisters Karen and Mary helped me organize and host a wonderful birthday party with all of his friends. I wanted to help mark the occasion by having him call his mother. I had remembered the anguish I had endured, especially during holidays and special events. But inflicting the same thing on his mother was not my style. He hadn't asked to talk to her, but I didn't feel that I should be an obstacle for contact with her either.

On the eve of his birthday I called Xalapa. Silvia answered the phone. We spoke in Spanish, and she openly wept while I explained what I had in mind.

BROKEN TREATY

"Look, Silvia, I'm not sure what your long range plans are involving Stephen's life, but I think it would mean a lot to Stephen to talk to him on his birthday tomorrow night," I said.

"I can't come back to California. They will put me in jail," she reasoned.

I was firm in my resolve.

"Until you decide what you are going to do, I would appreciate it if you could make any call to him as pleasant as possible." I asked.

Placing calls to Mexico rather than receiving them would not guarantee that my calls couldn't be traced, but it would make it more difficult. The night of his birthday, Stephen and his mother spoke for the first time in five months. The call was expectedly emotional, but surprisingly upbeat. The call seemed to give hope that neither would remain only voices from the other's past. There was a brief pause when she realized that he was only responding in English.

"When are you coming home, Mom?" Stephen asked.

"I can't be with you right now Son," was all that she would offer regarding her plans.

I had no way to be certain, but her tone seemed to suggest a status quo, indicating she had no plans to return to California.

About this time, Stephen had his last counseling visit and I was asked to have a seat while the two counselors rendered their opinion. "We don't find any immediate issues with Stephen regarding the drama from Mexico or his adjustment since returning home. He is socially adjusted, loves school and sports," the first counselor concluded.

"You haven't seen anything to worry about for now?" I asked.

"We think that you need to relax and let him just go on living the life of an 8-year-old boy. It also might be a good idea for you to seek some counseling at some point – based on what you've been through," the woman offered.

Two things struck me as I left that office with Stephen: I'd perhaps been over sensitive about his psyche; and that I may have had the first known encounter with psychologists not recommending a calendar full of return visits.

That week had been kind. I received news through Melanie from the D.A. that Mexico City had been told to "go pound sand" – that after review the D.A.'s office was refusing to prosecute. I was never given any specifics of the charges by Mexico, but Melanie had reasonable suspicion that a Mexican federal warrant for my arrest had been handed down and advised me to avoid traveling to or through Mexico—for the rest of my life.

I found it amusing how Mexico City had rallied to become so efficient when it came to pursuing me across the border with prosecution, but so blatantly incompetent in applying the law designed to spare parents this same fate. A little money and any attorney could tie a child's return until local courts deemed a return harmful to the child after a year. I did find over time that the U.S. also had a poor track record for international abduction returns. The figures are so distorted that relevant numbers are nearly impossible to come by. Ratios fluctuate wildly depending on the source. I refused to be bitter toward Mexico or the State Department, only disappointed that no one could tell me early on that my chances of recovering my son through legal channels were roughly one in a thousand.

I saw only positive consequences from the contact with Stephen and his mother. He seemed content with the occasional Sunday night calls. The cost of the calls limited the duration and the frequency of his conversations with his Mom, though he didn't seem anxious to know when they would talk again. Silvia was a little taken aback that Stephen spoke only English and while she did speak Spanish to him at the onset, he asked her to speak to him in English. I knew firsthand the crushing impact of your child suddenly not speaking the tongue you last spoke to them in. I had held out hope that their conversations would compel him to speak in Spanish, but he preferred to respond in English. Spanish was one benefit from his time in Mexico, but now he refused to speak it. I continued speaking to him in Spanish, but only privately now as it embarrassed him in front of his friends.

Through the first full year of his return to life at home, school and friends, I saw that there were fewer insecurity issues with Stephen. Since the occasional telephone dialogue with his mother began, he grew less reliant on holding my hand. Still, we continued to be careful about his safety. The staff at his school was vigilant and I became convinced that short of moving away, we were fairly secure. At 8 years old, he was still vulnerable, but the contact with his mother seemed to give him some confidence. If she chose to stay in Xalapa, perhaps understanding that he was thriving here with occasional access, might make her less inclined do something radical.

Soccer season had been a good one for Stephen, with him becoming one of the top players on his team. He performed well at any position from goalie to forward. When baseball tryouts began the following winter, he again expressed reservations about the new sport, but honored our agreement for two weeks of practice before

BROKEN TREATY

making a decision. Our informal throwing and batting over the summer had paid off and he could see the reaction and approval from the drafting coaches at tryouts.

On the way home, as he had done after his first soccer meeting, Stephen declared that baseball was worth pursuing.

"I saw some of the other players with some baseball gloves and bats I've never seen before, Dad. I think we should find out where we can buy them!" he informed.

Soccer was uncomplicated and the gear relatively inexpensive. Baseball equipment was another matter and before long Stephen was asking for a hundred dollar bat even though his age group only let coaches slow pitch to their own players.

As in soccer, Stephen excelled. He also was becoming a fan of any sport offered on television. Nothing was as exciting to him, however, as going to see the Giants play at home in San Francisco. My parents had season tickets to Giants games nearly every season and he got to see as many games as we could get to; even getting to meet players and tour the dugout – something arranged by his aunt Mary.

With the inclusion of basketball, Stephen was now occupied 10 months of each year with sports. His soccer coach gradually developed a select team that included Stephen in an exclusive league, which meant extensive travel for tournaments. I was asked to be the assistant coach. I accepted the appointment and I got to experience first-hand the wrath of parents demanding to know why their child wasn't in the game at any given moment. The team performed well in its division and the parents seemed to enjoy the social aspects of overnight tournament trips as much as the boys.

BROKEN TREATY

While school and sports occupied Stephens social calendar during most of the year, we began jet skiing regularly during the summer on a second-hand, two-seat Sea-Doo that I bought. When we tired of the smaller local reservoirs, we ventured further out to the larger lakes. Stephen became a skilled rider, though he was constantly chasing the minimum age limit to ride alone. As the sport grew in popularity so did the speed of water craft and fatalities soared. The minimum age for single riders with no adult increased from 12 to 16 years of age in a few short years. Stephen had become a better jetski pilot than any adult I'd ever seen. On warm quiet evenings just before sunset and after the sheriffs pulled their boats out of the water, I'd let Stephen have at it on the lake by himself, with the consolation that he knew the regulations and was trained to constantly scan all directions with an eagle eye for hazards and other boats.

After more than two years of only phone contact with his mother, it became clear that she had no intention of returning to face the felony charges pending in California. I never got any impression that Silvia was even remotely remorseful about hiding our son. Her pride was an obsession. Silvia's father, Alberto, had died the past year, yet he never made any effort to visit or even talk to his grandson. I believed that his silence was simply a matter of pride – even at the cost of never hearing his grandson's voice or seeing him one last time. Mexican culture would not allow him to appear submissive, preferring instead to remain mortally offended by the rescue. While the complications of diabetes accelerated his demise, I believe Alberto died in part from a broken heart for the devastation he helped bring to his favorite daughter.

BROKEN TREATY

If the calls with his mom had a positive effect, I wondered if there would be any harm in a face-to-face visit with his mother at the border. This would have to take place at a location where Stephen and Silvia could have some kind of visual and verbal access, but also where I did not have to worry about him being snatched.

San Ysidro is a small California community south of San Diego that abuts the Mexican border. I called a relative who happened to be an immigration attorney living in the San Diego area. I explained what I had in mind.

"Border Park in Imperial Beach would be perfect. It has a single cyclone fence that drops directly into the ocean between Mexico and California. I've seen people gather and talk through the fence with no hassles from the Border Patrol, but they watch every move you make," he told me.

I mentioned the idea to Silvia to see if she might be interested in a border fence visit. She was willing to fly to Tijuana and could arrange to stay with relatives. I asked Stephen how he felt about such a visit. His eyes grew wide at the prospect of seeing his mom, even under the limited conditions.

"What if someone tries to take me back to Mexico," he countered.

At that moment I knew that he was going to make this decision without my influence.

"I won't let anything happen to you of course, but the entire decision is yours. If you decide to do this and it doesn't look right when we get there, we turn around and go home. I just want you to know that I might have this figured out if you want to give it a try," I said.

BROKEN TREATY

Stephen's soccer prowess grows as he matures.

BROKEN TREATY

Chapter 26

A Visit Through the Border Fence

Interstate 5 is a virtual parking lot through Los Angeles and traffic doesn't subside until 9:00 p.m. The freeway meanders two more hours through San Diego, then just 18 miles more to the Mexican border town of Tijuana.

The sign for the last U.S. exit is clearly marked. Still, I nearly drove past it and into Mexico by mistake near midnight. I hadn't been to the border since Silvia and I used to cross over into Tijuana to park-n-fly out of the airport to save on airfare to Mexico City. I hadn't anticipated my own uneasiness being this close to Mexico. My heart rate was erratic until I got us turned around headed north and put a couple of exits between us and the international line. I found a modest but clean motel that worked into our budget for the next few days.

After getting Stephen comfortable for the night, I sat back in my bed looking over the details for the next morning. I had a meeting at 9 a.m. in town with a licensed bodyguard. I had to pay cash for two six-hour shifts for him to watch over us at Border Field Park. I realized this was drastic, but I was willing to accept appearing paranoid for peace of mind.

Even at 1:00 a.m., Stephen was unable to get to sleep.

"Do you think Mom will start to cry when we see her tomorrow, Dad?"

This was a good question. Two and a half years had passed since the rescue. My initial anger from the abduction itself had grown into pity; then back to anger again at her refusal to handle her problems for Stephen's sake. Her actions were nothing more than "narcissism on parade." If anyone cared to know, I suppose I had come full circle back to pity.

"You know, Son, your Mom will probably cry, but I think it will be a happy kind of cry. I think that she'll be so glad to see you that it won't be long before she is smiling and laughing," I suggested.

Family and friends were perplexed by my making this trip with Stephen, though no one came right out to tell me it was a bad idea. I was acting on a strange impulse, feeling somehow virtuous about the visit. But as far as I was concerned, our parental feelings were irrelevant. This was all about Stephen.

The sheer size of the man seated opposite me at the desk was impressive. He was no less than six-and-a-half feet tall, but with a disproportionate girth at no less than 400 pounds. Yet this giant hardly appeared threatening as he wiped both eyes before I finished telling him why we were in town. Stephen, meanwhile, busied himself with a few San Diego Padres souvenirs that the man had given him.

"The layout at Border Field Park is straight forward. A simple cyclone fence will let them talk as long as they want," the massive guard said.

"To be honest with you, I'm more concerned about him being pulled or taken into Mexico from someone on this side. The Border Patrol could care less about anyone going into Mexico. I don't want

BROKEN TREATY

anyone near us." I told him.

He seemed sympathetic to my paranoia and opened a top desk drawer, revealing a Berreta pistol, with others. The giant slapped a clip into the bottom of the pistol butt then eyed me for a reaction. The overdramatic effect caused me to turn to see if Stephen had witnessed the man's action. I sought a gun licensed body-guard, but assumed more discretion for Stephen's sake. Two hours later we returned to the industrial office park location to follow our behemoth guardian's car to Border Field Park.

The Friday afternoon's light off-shore breeze helped moderate the summer heat. Finding Mexico at Border Field Park is as easy as looking toward the beach and then turning your head to the left. Silvia was out in the open several yards from where the steel fence panels stopped at the bottom of the hillside – permanent reminders of the political geography between the two countries. Two hundred yards of relatively unobtrusive interwoven wire mesh offered a limited panorama into Mexican real estate before returning back to solid fence panels toward the water where the final 250 yards of solid barrier ran down the beach, disappearing into the surf.

Stephen saw his mother before we parked. She was the only person at the 100-yard section of see-through cyclone fencing. I moved slowly, helping Stephen gather some things he'd brought as gifts for his Mom, giving our bodyguard time to get ahead of us. Stephen kept an even pace as we made our way over the Bermuda grass turf. Each step forward created a wider angled view into Mexico. A large bullfight ring across the street on the Mexican side filled much of the background, and I saw no menacing characters looming about. She had a surprisingly short hair style.

BROKEN TREATY

"Mom," Stephen called out, his voice was cheerful, yet casual as though returning for lunch from a long hike. The two pressed their palms together between the weaving of the cyclone wire. Silvia's face broadened into a spontaneous smile. Her euphoria overcame any inclination to weep. The emotion of the moment was surreal.

An outsider, given any background on the meeting, would be hard pressed to understand the absence of bitterness. But I believed we'd all put too much effort and traveled too far to see any value in hostility. Even the language issue had resolved itself, with Silvia dusting off her English.

"My God, Stephen," she declared. "You are so tall now. I can't believe you are so big."

Hearing those words from a mother to her child through a cyclone fence reminded me of how complicated our lives had become.

Stephen began sorting through the gifts of photos and sweets he'd brought her. Only a few yards away, we found a face-size hole that allowed a volley of the harmless gifts back and forth. The exchange was so heavy, in fact, that our bodyguard was now fielding questions from a U.S. Border Patrol officer who had quietly driven up behind us in a green and white truck. I watched our monster friend brief the agent on our business at the fence and the Border Patrol agent apparently was satisfied because he drove away. I assumed every move we made was observed by agents as well as by remote surveillance. Hopefully, the officer we'd just encountered would tell others that our business was lawful.

I moved away to take some pictures of the two and give them time to talk alone. When I saw a pause, I rallied Stephen to show off some of his baseball skills with the gear I'd brought with us.

BROKEN TREATY

Stephen's ball skills impressed his Mom, prompting a "wow" or "oh my God" comment with nearly every snapping catch or return throw. After a rest, and more talking, we alternated to passing a soccer ball, then a Frisbee. There was a profound sense of pride in wanting to share his sport skills and techniques while his Mom took photos. I had the sense that she had not been aware of his athletic talents.

We shared soft drinks and treats through the fence, but didn't get hassled by the Border Patrol. We'd been left alone. After four hours of visiting, I became comfortable enough to suggest to our bodyguard that we wouldn't need him the next day. The sweat drenched man had no quarrel with the idea, conceding that the border agents were an even greater deterrent than he was at this point. We wound up the end of the first day's visit with everyone happy, but anxious to get some shade. We would meet again at 10 the next morning.

There was no mistake: Stephen not only enjoyed the visit with his mother, he seemed to understand and accept the complexities of the arrangement. He also seemed sincerely grateful that it had all come together. He'd never changed his feelings for his mother; rather, he had simply adjusted to the situation the best he could. He never put blame on the foolishness of his parents.

Only 30 minutes into the visit with Stephen and Silvia at the fence the next morning, two television media vans drove into the park. The vans parked adjacent to us and television people piled out. Silvia gave me a bitter scowl as though I was behind this, assuming I had exploited our visit. The look from her dismissed my counter accusation, realizing it wasn't likely this was something she could have arranged from Mexico. I remembered that the Republican National Convention was winding up in San Diego. The group must have been looking for a border related story with reporters in front of cameras pointed in our direction. She wouldn't accept my theory, believing that I was behind it even after they scattered 30 minutes later, leaving Border Field Park just as abruptly as they had come.

In the mid afternoon of the third and last day, while at the fence, I turned to see a woman Border Patrol official walking toward us from her truck parked down the dirt path. The Border Patrol vehicles are stealthy, with only the sound of knobby tires rolling through the fine beach sand. She walked our way purposefully, and I moved to meet her half way. I worried that the agent's interest would needlessly reaffirm the bleakness of this aspect in Stephen's life. I tried to offer just enough to satisfy her—"just my son visiting his mother." Instead, she began probing.

"I've been watching a lot of things being passed through the fence which is illegal. Why can't she visit, or you two visit her in Mexico?" she questioned. She looked past me, eyeing them both, but listened intently to the details. Silvia glanced twice in my direction, to measure the woman's reaction, but the agent had none, only watching as I explained why none of us could step across the other's border. She was tall and fit with a ponytail of long dark hair pulled through the back of her uniform cap. She wore aviator glasses that obscured her eyes, just two feet from my face. After 30 seconds of silence, not knowing what to expect, a tear appeared on her left cheek, just below her sunglasses. I wished I hadn't seen it, fearing she might have to counter her sensitivity with a harsh reaction.

"Enjoy your visit. No one else will bother you today," the Border Patrol officer said.

She turned, walked back to her truck, climbed into the cab and in reverse gear, disappeared back down the dusty trail as silently as she had come upon us.

The day's shadows crept eastward, a reminder of the night's 400-mile drive ahead. Work was to be reckoned with in the morning. Stephen said goodbye to his mother, but soon after reaching the highway, he grew quiet. I didn't try to impose my analysis of the weekend visit or revisit the potential of his mom's return. Everything was exactly the way it was supposed to be. His mother seemed resolved to staying in Mexico and neither Stephen nor I speculated when or even if another visit at the border was in the future.

BROKEN TREATY

Under the watchful eye of Border Patrol agents, Stephen and Silvia visit through the cyclone fence on the border between Chula Vista and Tijuana.

Chapter 27

Silvia returns to face the music

There were two more visits with Stephen and his mom at the border cyclone fence over the next 14 months. While Stephen looked forward to the trips, I began to see that Silvia seemed content with the visits, not even discussing a remedy for her situation. The D.A.'s policy for child abduction was clear: no plea bargaining on child abduction charges while a fugitive. She must return to California to be booked and answer the charges.

The D.A. was willing to offer 48 hours to surrender, allowing her to clear immigration on entry to the United States. Silvia had enlisted the pro-bono help of a local prominent attorney she found on the internet who had begun a dialogue with me and the D.A.'s office. Melanie Headrick was adamant that I had little influence with the prosecution. The charges had been filed along with the arrest warrant and bail set at $500,000 five years previous. The same prosecutor and staff were still at their posts as the case file began to see new activity.

In June of 1998, five and a half years after Silvia had left California with our Son, she landed at San Francisco International Airport from Mexico City. Stephen had flowers for his mom as we greeted her outside of the customs exit. I was excited for Stephen as the two hugged this time without a border barrier between them. Silvia's female attorney had sent an office assistant and a driver to greet her at the airport. They assumed that only hostility existed and couldn't understand what I was doing at the airport with Stephen. I

BROKEN TREATY

let it be their problem and the confusion was handled. Stephen and I would drive his mother to San Jose for a meeting at her attorney's office. Stephen grinned ear to ear as he and his mother laughed and caught up with each other's lives. Stephen and I waited outside while his mother managed her legal affairs with the lawyer.

In the afternoon, the three of us grabbed a late lunch at an empty Mexican restaurant. I intruded little during this reunion, and only offered a positive playful tone when I saw fit to interject. We didn't discuss her impending surrender to authorities planned the next day in front of Stephen, but I volunteered to help out by taking her down to the county jail and stay with her as long as the booking process would permit. This was a long time coming. She was understandably terrified even though unofficial indications were that she would be incarcerated overnight only with bail dismissed and an arraignment scheduled.

I took a call from Melanie while I walked from the jail house to the parking lot.

"Steve, the prosecutor doesn't consider the victim's opinion in these cases, but off the record—if you had any say in this, would you want to see this pursued under felony charges or dropped down to misdemeanor?" Melanie asked directly.

The question caught me off balance. I didn't want my personal input to be a factor either way, yet part of me saw the merit of what I could do with my vote as far as Stephen's long-term welfare and self esteem were concerned.

"What's the bottom line either way?"

"A felony conviction will follow her for life, making it hard to find work and probably six months to a year in county jail. A

BROKEN TREATY

misdemeanor child abduction conviction would most likely only be the time served until she is released tomorrow with two years probation. She would most likely have to pay some restitution in either case," she answered.

Melanie knew my answer before she even made the call.

"Look, I can't see any good coming from Stephen seeing his mother go to jail. She is the other half of everything he is. I'd like to see the charges reduced to misdemeanor for Stephen."

By the end of our call, I had an impression that felony charges would be substituted for misdemeanors. Nothing more could be offered on my part. The decision of what to do with her was beyond my control. I could at least feel good about what I tried to do when asked on Stephen's behalf.

A year before Silvia's return to California, Stephen and I had moved to Danville, east and inland from San Francisco Bay. I had been able to get a foothold in the area with some remodeling projects that generated enough word-of-mouth business that I was able to eventually wind up business 30 miles south in San Jose and focus on an eager customer base in Danville. Stephen had finished fifth grade at his new elementary school, and was ready for junior high. He'd made lots of new friends and was popular with students and teammates in soccer and baseball. He not only played well at the two sports, but had aspirations of moving up into the local select soccer division and the majors for his age group in baseball. I was fortunate that, no matter where we ended up, he found an allure in sports, minimizing his internet surfing and computer gaming. Most evenings after practice or games, he just didn't have the energy to do much beyond homework or limited computer play, which helped limit the time he had to get into trouble.

The charges against Silvia were eventually reduced to misdemeanor. I saw no need to mention my conversation with Melanie, or suggest to Stephen that I had any influence on the prosecution's new position. I was no longer involved, and didn't probe for details. I was only happy for Stephen to see that the absence of his mother in his life had come to an end.

From her first night out of jail, Silvia lived in the home of her woman attorney in a secluded, wooded area of the Santa Cruz Mountains, a small range that separates the Pacific Coast from Silicon Valley. Silvia had no transportation, but occasionally was able to borrow a car. When she couldn't I drove Stephen up the mountain to see his mother and occasionally take her out for excursions. I played hooky from work one day to trailer our two jet skis up the mountain to take Silvia and her attorney's daughter to the reservoir for the day. Stephen was anxious to show off his jet ski handling skills to his mom seated behind him, unaware of the terror it would inflict on her. When Stephen returned to the beach with the jet ski – his mom's face was white with fear.

As the weeks of summer wore on, I found myself with less time to drive Stephen to visit his mother. I had become engaged to marry Ann, a woman I had met nearly two years previously. She had been raising three younger children on her own, two girls and a baby boy. The six of us were now under one-roof and the kids seemed to get along. Stephen, over time, moved into the older brother role. We had considered some elaborate places to wed, but settled on sprucing up the home for a ceremony and reception that was kinder to our budget.

BROKEN TREATY

The kids had met Silvia and they all seemed exceedingly tolerant of one another. When Silvia was able to borrow a car, I made her welcome at our home to visit Stephen. His schedule with weekend soccer games offered great opportunities to see him play and spend time with him. Into the fall and approaching four months after her return, I developed confidence with her movement toward resolving her legal issues. Though not plugged in to details of her proceedings, I quietly wondered how she had been able to continue to have the hearings repeatedly continued and extended. The matter was not my concern, so I didn't worry a great deal about it.

I began letting Silvia share Stephen's bedroom for overnight stays at our home. Although Stephen was 12 and taller than his mother by now, I only found peace those nights by discreetly moving one of our vehicles behind hers in the driveway. This made it impossible for her to drive off with Stephen while I slept.

We invited her to stay with us for Christmas. Early on Christmas Eve I invited Silvia for a drink and we ended up cheering Christmas together at the bar of a local restaurant. I entertained her with a little humor and saw that she seemed unguarded. I'd not had a private moment with her since before she had taken Stephen, to Mexico, six years before. I felt that I was somehow entitled to ask a burning question.

"Silvia, you've never given me a straight answer to why you took Stephen. Can you please tell me why you did it?"

The lighthearted atmosphere vaporized.

"It's complicated and I don't want to talk about it," she declared, severing eye contact.

Her reaction had been the same when we walked along the beach that morning so many years ago in Veracruz when I confided that her father tried to buy me a hooker after dismissing the family at dinner in the restaurant. I knew her well enough that she wouldn't even bother trying to make something up to satisfy me. She wasn't talking and I would never get an answer.

Before we left the bar, she asked if I'd consider dropping the $80,000 awarded to me from our divorce for legal expenses encountered in trying to recover Stephen and the cost of the rescue itself. I had no intention of releasing that obligation, but I was amused at her timing, after refusing to offer any reason why she had hidden Stephen in Mexico.

From outward appearances, it looked like I was doing well financially. We lived in an upscale neighborhood, I'd had a custom-built truck for the business shipped from Detroit and a crew of three fulltime employees. I also had a pleased customer base that was providing plenty of referrals. I'd been able to take Ann to Hawaii for our honeymoon. Between Ann's resources and mine, she was able to stay at home as a homemaker. I still owed a small fortune to my family and had made slow, but steady progress to meet those obligations. Silvia had no way of knowing the fine line between our current prosperity and struggling to make ends meet. She had convinced herself that I could absorb the loss of her court sanctioned reimbursement to me. I didn't know if Silvia would ever come across any significant money to settle, but there was no good argument to dismiss it either.

Ann went to great lengths to make Silvia's first Christmas in four years with her son as pleasant as possible. Everybody in the family wanted her to feel included, almost as part of an extended family.

BROKEN TREATY

There were gifts under the tree for her from each of us. Yet I could feel resentment from Silvia since the drink at the bar. She, of course, was there for Stephen and only tolerated the rest of us. I'd had no reason to expect anything beyond that, but the kids offered innocent kindness, happy for Stephen that he could be with his mom and trying to make her feel at home. Stephen seemed to understand this best and appreciated our efforts. He was brimming with pride, having access to both parents for the first time since we'd split up when he was 4. There wasn't much in his life to complain about these days.

During the holidays, while Stephen's soccer season had ended and baseball wouldn't be starting up until February, I grew confident enough to let Stephen travel with his mother for an occasional weekend at the home where she lived with the woman attorney in the Santa Cruz Mountains. I'd had a long discussion with the woman who assured me that Stephen would be safe in her home and that Silvia's passport had been surrendered as a condition of her release from jail until the sentencing hearing. Stephen's age and size alone suggested that another abduction would not be possible.

On a late Sunday afternoon of February 14, my wife and I drove to San Jose to pick up Stephen from a weekend with his mother. Before parting, Silvia handed us a Valentine's Day card with two candy lollipops. There was something strange about the offering.

BROKEN TREATY

Chapter 28

No good deed goes unpunished

At 7:00 a.m., two days after I'd last seen Silvia on Valentine's Day, I responded to an aggressive knock on the door. A large man asked my name; handed me a set of papers, turned and walked away. The man was a process server. Anxiety took hold as I began to understand the document's significance. I was being summoned to answer to a custody motion for Stephen by his mother. I realized almost immediately that this was the same morning that she was being sentenced for child stealing in Santa Clara County Criminal Court.

The core premise of paperwork included a very meticulously documented log of Stephen's visits with his mother. I was to appear in Santa Clara Family Court in two-and-a half weeks to respond. Not even Stephen had been aware of his mother's intentions. I was mortified and Ann felt hurt by the aggression. This dust wasn't going to settle anytime soon. My only recourse now was to contact my former attorney Brad Baugh and ask if he'd represent me again while figuring out how to come up with his retainer.

"No good deed goes unpunished," were Brad's first words. "I just have to say that giving your ex-wife access to your son after abducting him to Mexico was about the stupidest thing I've seen in my career. What the hell were you thinking?" he demanded rhetorically.

Brad pulled no punches in criticizing my poor judgment. Any good intentions were completely canceled out by Silvia's calculated assumptions of my nearsightedness.

The only consolation that I found was that Silvia's attorney; who was also her host and landlord, somehow overlooked that fact that we hadn't lived in Santa Clara County for nearly a year-and-a-half.

Baugh had the case dismissed in court in Santa Clara, but it was moved up to Contra Costa Family Court jurisdiction. Baugh told me that I was on my own as he didn't know that court and the travel didn't make any sense for either of us.

I interviewed several recommended attorneys. I settled for one that Baugh had referred. He seemed sharp and the word was that the judges respected him. He also was one of the most expensive attorneys in the county. I had to pay his retainer with a credit card. Silvia also had asked the court to mandate an "anger management evaluation" for me with a court approved psychologist with absolutely no basis or specific allegation. The evaluator found no grounds for further evaluation after a one-time visit, but it was another cost among others that continued to pile up. Silvia asked for a court-appointed interpreter even though she was fully fluent in English and had completed two years of college level studies at San Jose State University in computer science engineering. Plus, she now had a fulltime job in the high tech industry

Once more Stephen was in the middle of this mess seeing how the legal assault was stressing me. He even told me that he'd asked his mom to drop the action as he didn't want to miss the time on the field with his teammates in soccer and baseball from having to travel for visitation. It took all the resolve I could manage to keep from sharing how I felt about his mother and what a mistake I'd made. The only thing that kept me from downloading was the

BROKEN TREATY

pledge I made long ago not to smear his mother in a personal attack for her actions that he had no control over.

It took about three months for the case to be heard again in the new venue. My new attorney was masterful, delivering a compelling argument that Silvia had "unclean hands" regarding the initial abduction and that until she could establish other entitlement, Stephen's legal and physical custody should remain with me. The court had determined that travel to the Santa Cruz Mountains would be too disruptive, keeping visitation in Danville for Silvia on alternate Saturday and Sunday two-hour weekend visits with me supervising until she could have a court approved supervisor to monitor visitation. Before the hearing was completed, however, the judge gave Silvia a scathing lecture on her abduction of Stephen to Mexico, pointing out that she clearly demonstrated no remorse for her actions.

Nearly as soon as the awkwardness of court ordered visitation appeared to become routine, I found myself again responding to motions back in court with Silvia trying to gain some form of custody. My attorney's fees kept us barely able to pay my bills while Silvia enjoyed bottomless legal representation from her connections. My family was sympathetic to my dilemma, but never quite figured out why I had been so intent on helping Silvia back into Stephen's life.

As Stephen grew older, it became harder to convince the court that his mother continued to be a threat by taking him back to Mexico. Silvia had married a man who had become the visitation supervisor. Even though there was no established unsupervised visitation, Silvia and her new husband had moved into a rental home only a few blocks away in our neighborhood. It was at this time that I began to see a major disruption in our home with Stephen choosing to distance himself from the family.

I found myself now served with documents notifying me that Silvia had filed for bankruptcy. There was still the issue of the $80,000 she owed from the divorce, but that would be washed away. My attorney suggested that I hire a bankruptcy attorney to challenge her debt absolution in court; however, another attorney's retainer was beyond our budget. I was forced to make decisions on what was worth throwing toward the good fight and what was unsalvageable. Silvia had a lot to offer her son with few financial demands of her own. As he grew older and drawn more toward his mother, I could only hope that the time I'd fought so hard to keep him under my roof would establish some of the virtues that I'd tried to instill in him—maybe not to surface until he was a young man.

Animosity was slowly developing between Stephen and Ann's girls. I discovered that he'd snuck out of the house a couple of times after midnight and was starting to get into trouble at school. I had never exacted any kind of physical punishment, but one afternoon after learning from a parent that he'd been terrorizing a classmate with developmental challenges, I blew my top and charged at Stephen, giving him a healthy shove in front of two friends while playing basketball in our backyard. My regretful act was partially out of rage—and in some measure, an attempt to intentionally humiliate him as a lesson. He retaliated with a verbal assault that only escalated as his friends stood watching.

Unskilled at managing teenage rage, I sought to counter his foul-mouthed disrespect by bringing out the boxing gloves. My approach was simple: he would have the right to talk disrespectfully

BROKEN TREATY

if he could earn it by out-boxing me; and in the worst case scenario, he'd learn some defensive skills. He refused to pick up the gloves, instead choosing to isolate himself from me. My judgment had fault.

With no better back-up plan, I arranged a series of counseling appointments for us. After an evaluation with weeks of sessions, the therapist made the radical suggestion of enrolling Stephen in another high school with a closed campus for lunch, and a more economically modest student body. The therapist believed that the local high school students were spoiled brats who drank only the best alcohol and smoked the finest pot. With the opinion of a skilled child behavior expert, how could I go wrong?

During his freshman year at his new school, the court determined that his mother would have unsupervised visits on alternate weekends. He did insist on not leaving town with her on weekends because of his games. Baseball had been abandoned, but he poured his heart into soccer with such passion that his coach asked him to become captain of the junior varsity soccer team as a freshman. School and soccer kept him busy and tired. Although at his mom's two weekends each month, the stillness of his bedroom was dramatic and I never fully came to terms that he was getting old enough to start making decisions about where he wanted to be. There was a tear in the family fabric in our home.

I didn't back off on certain demands and expectations with Stephen when it came to school, chores and social behavior. I wasn't around to be his best friend. I realized that I was the one person in his life who was going to be tough on him. Silvia obviously couldn't say "no."

BROKEN TREATY

We still did outings as a family when he was not with his mother. But he always returned home from weekends with his Mom bringing an attitude that grew progressively worse. For the first time in his life, Stephen seemed uncaring of others and insensitive to my feelings about his detachment.

During the summer, before the beginning of his junior year on a family jetski trip, the pin finally came out of the hinge. When I complained to Stephen about not helping load the jet skis onto the trailer, he unleashed a verbal tirade on the family and called Ann a "fucking bitch." I became furious and indicated that he would go to stay with my sister Mary until he could apologize. The apology didn't come, and after four nights at my sister's house he went to live with his mother.

I was taken back into court by his mother now for monthly child support. The $2,000 per month support order based on my previous year's income was a tough hit, and the economy had just started to slow. There was a backlash from bad mortgage loans, freezing home equity lines of credit for many homeowners that now found themselves owing more on their properties than they were worth.

I found it harder to manage the household single handedly, and Ann saw that there was no other choice but to re-enter the job market. She found work at a nearby elementary school as a teacher's aide. The pay and health benefits were welcome help.

I secretly held out hope that Stephen would get over the issues that drove him away and come back home. His empty bedroom was a painful reminder. I did my best to control my bitterness toward his mother, realizing that character attacks on her would only drive Stephen and me further apart. At 16, my son was old enough to make the choice to live with his mother. Although she never expressed any kind of atonement for hiding him in Mexico, she at least feared his displeasure. My strongest reservation was that her guilt-fueled inability to say "no" or to establish any meaningful boundaries for him would ruin his character.

I believed that I'd lost my parental foothold. The best I could hope for was that my firm guidance would eventually take hold in him. Silvia enjoyed the physical custody of Stephen along with the revenue that came with it. All I could do was accept that I no longer had control.

In his junior year, Stephen was drafted to an elite soccer team, independent of the high school league. Each player had been hand-picked and practices were coached with the help of a veteran pro-soccer player with the Los Angeles Clash. Selection for the team was his proudest accomplishment, escalating the self-esteem of an already confident young man. The team practices alone were a thrill, motivating me to shorten my work day now and then to attend. Only three weeks into the season, Stephen lost his footing in a sharp cut on the turf, tearing bone fragments in his left ankle. I shared his heartbreak, realizing that the season was lost for him, but relieved to see he was destined for a full recovery.

When the cast was finally removed and the added time to regain full strength in his ankle factored-in, other sports at school had no appeal to him. We began motocross riding in the hills outside Livermore at Carnegie on weekends. The reluctance of his mother to try to manage his schedule had at least surfaced as an unforeseen advantage. In the summers he worked with me in my business and we jetskied on weekends at our favorite lakes in California's Central

BROKEN TREATY

Valley whenever we could get free. One of our most memorable adventures came when we were playing hooky one April weekday morning. We jet skied for an hour at Folsom Lake then trailered the jetskis to Heavenly Valley and were on the slopes with our skis and snowboard by 2:00 p.m. the same day.

Sadly our one-on-one time began to dissolve when his mother and her new husband bought him a BMW. Not long after getting the car, he became less available. Motocross, jetskiing and snowboarding were now just good memories. A couple of weeks after he got the car, Ann came upon the Highway Patrol lecturing Stephen. He had lost control of the car on a freeway on-ramp and had spun out. I had been rendered a spectator. There was no dialogue between his mother and me. Stephen wanted to continue working for me for extra spending money, but now that he had his own car, the theory was that he would drive himself to my job sites. Instead he became less reliable, showing up hours late or at times not at all. For a time I drove to his mother's house to get him out of bed. Eventually I lost patience and stopped going to get him.

His last year of high school was painful to witness. There was no interest in sports or activities (except computers) and toward the end of the year he saw little value in attending classes. Beginning the school year as an adult, no parent was required to be notified of tardiness or class cuts. His senior year was like a cruise ship vacation.

Except for a glove box full of traffic violations, Stephen had been smart enough to stay out of trouble with the authorities. He knew when not to pop off or push his luck. I kept hearing stories about him getting in fist fights at parties, sometimes with his best

BROKEN TREATY

friends.

A few weeks before the end of his senior year, in danger of not graduating, Stephen's friends began pressuring him to make his classes. They didn't want to see him left behind. They seemed to know in their hearts that Stephen had a future – if he would only work for it. They literally walked him to class every morning during the last weeks of school.

Not until a few days before graduation did he receive notice that he could graduate with the rest of the class. Every senior in his class accepted their diploma with pride, but perhaps the young man who had taunted the system was the most grateful recipient of the San Ramon Valley High School class of 2005. Stephen caught me alone before heading off to celebrate. With pride and a flicker of maturity he handed me his diploma, moving me near tears.

A week later found Stephen for the first time in 11 years back in Mexico on his senior graduation trip to Cancun. I wondered if he might get hassled by Mexican officials due to upgrades in computerized immigration screening because of our common names. I'd never been able to get confirmation that Mexican authorities were no longer interested in me.

BROKEN TREATY

BROKEN TREATY

CHAPTER 29

STEPHEN'S REVELATION

Stephen suddenly become ambitious about college as he watched his friends preparing for the fall semester. His grade-point-average was weak, so he decided he would start at ground zero in the community college system. Santa Barbara was his choice for a junior college because it offered a path directly into the University of California at Santa Barbara. I hadn't anticipated this kind of forward thinking on his part, but was thrilled to see ambition with a college theme.

Even though he'd turned 18 the year before, I was obligated to continue paying his mother the $2000/month child support until he graduated from high school. Now, I had confidence that my help would not be supporting his mother's household. I had created my problems by helping his mother back into his life, but the financial challenges had created friction between Ann and me.

In September of 2008, we split so abruptly that I didn't have a place to live. But I had promised Stephen I would drive to Santa Barbara to be with him on his 22nd birthday. I would worry about a new home when I got back. He'd asked me to take him to the California Adventure Park at Disneyland for the day – just the two of us.

Stephen drove us to the park that Friday morning – a day when the lines are shorter. The day was his and I was eager to spoil him, but I was surprised to discover that he was worried about me being alone.

BROKEN TREATY

He selected a table for two at a restaurant and the conversation was light hearted, mostly small talk about the family and his new place in Santa Barbara, where he was in his third year at college.

"Dad, I know I've never really mentioned it, but I want you to know that I understand what you went through to find me and bring me home when mom took me to Mexico and decided to keep me there," he said.

My heart skipped a beat while my throat swelled, leaving me speechless and unable to chew. A day hadn't passed since the drama so many years ago that I didn't think about what happened or the way things could have turned out. I pushed my sunglasses up the bridge of my nose to shield my eyes from the tears that now began to well. I had no way of knowing that this was coming. He continued: "Dad, I know that there aren't many fathers out there who would have even tried to do what you did even if they'd been in the same situation. Instead of giving up and going on with your life, you sacrificed everything and came for me. What made the ultimate difference is that although you didn't forgive my mom, you still helped bring her back into my life, because you knew what it meant to me," he explained.

"Instead of being grateful, she made you miserable again and I know that you began to regret it, thinking that you made a huge mistake. What I'm trying to tell you, Dad, is that it wasn't a mistake.

"Dad—I've seen the studies on the long term issues that abducted children go through later in life. You kept it from happening. Look at me! I wouldn't have this wonderful life and the opportunities in front of me if you hadn't done what you did. Thank you, Dad," he

BROKEN TREATY

said. His voice resonated with sincerity and a look in his big brown eyes that seemed beyond his years.

My eyes welled up and I could not speak.

I never anticipated this acknowledgement. I didn't know how to respond at the moment, but our lunch together that day was a turning point. His revelations were pivotal, and I was overcome with a strange peace. The acknowledgment from my son wasn't meant to be until now, when everything was exactly the way it was supposed to be.

Fourteen years after bringing my son home, he helped me understand that I could look ahead and realize that we'd both finally made it home.

BROKEN TREATY

Stephen snowboarding at Lake Tahoe in December of 2010.

BROKEN TREATY

EPILOGUE

I have stayed in touch with Melanie Headrick over the years. She retired from her position with the Santa Clara District Attorney's office and now lives south of San Jose, caring for her horses and traveling the world.

Pat Buckman disappeared into relative obscurity and seemed to erase his tracks. I was unable to turn up even a photograph or find any old news articles on him. I figured that he most likely prefers not having a bitter abducting parent with a long memory menacing him or his family. The last address I had for him was a Post Office box in Northern California.

My contact in Xalapa, who provided the information that made the rescue possible, is unwilling to talk to me or to anyone on my behalf, fearing retaliation.

I never tried to contact my attorney, Sr. Zurutusa, after he informed me that our conversation on the telephone was being tapped.

I had hoped that time would allow me to disclose the anonymous official that passed Buckman's name to me, but that individual prefers to leave things as they are. Even Stephen does not know the identify of this person.

There is one other name I would like to mention. This person was a client of mine and he provided helpful details on the plane we used to fly out of Xalapa and what the pilot was likely facing. Ten months after providing me with technical insight on this book, he saved 155 lives by putting a United Airlines A-320 passenger jet down on the Hudson River. His name is Capt. Sully Sullenberger.